PRODUCT PLANNING

PRODUCT PLANNING

An Integrated Approach

Merlin Stone, B.A., D.Phil.

Senior Lecturer,
School of Economics and Politics,
Kingston Polytechnic

A HALSTED PRESS BOOK

JOHN WILEY & SONS
New York

First published in the United Kingdom 1976 by
THE MACMILLAN PRESS LTD
London and Basingstoke

Published in the U.S.A.
by Halsted Press, a Division
of John Wiley & Sons, Inc.
New York

Printed in Great Britain

Library of Congress Cataloging in Publication Data
Stone, Merlin.
    Product planning, an integrated approach.
    "A Halsted Press book."
    1. Product management. I. Title.
HF5415.15.S76   1976   658.5'6   76-26335
ISBN 0-470-98915-7

To Ofra

Contents

List of Illustrations

Preface

This book arose out of my research on the product policies of industrial firms. As an economist, I had been struck by the extent to which economists had switched from studying price formation and associated problems to the study of the impact of other marketing variables, including product line policy, on the way in which firms in an industry interact. However, the importance of what could be called 'managerial variables' (which can be defined as variables which are not solely dependent on main line economic factors, such as costs, revenues, etc.) seemed to have been underrated in economists' writings on this topic. In my doctoral thesis, submitted at the University of Sussex, I tried to bring out the importance of these variables.

While I was carrying out this research and pursuing the appropriate reading, it became clear to me that there was no short, straightforward book available which put into perspective for the manager or the student of management the logical problems inherent in the product planning process, without getting bogged down in the details of certain techniques (which are of course changing all the time). This book represents an attempt to produce such a work.

My thanks are due to the Esmee Fairbairn Trust, for financing most of the research on which this book is based. Without their help, I should not have been able to interview the appropriate managers in thirty firms or to gather information on many more. Unfortunately, problems of confidentiality prevent any identification of these firms.

My thanks are also due to my supervisor in my doctoral studies, Professor Tibor Barna of the University of Sussex, for setting me on this line of research and for giving me encouragement when needed, to Professor Eric Shankleman of the Cranfield Institute of Technology for his comments on some of my work, and to the staff of the School of Business Administration, Hebrew University of Jerusalem, for research facilities and valuable comments. I am particularly grateful to Malcolm Cunningham, of the Department of Management Sciences, University of Manchester Institute of Science and Technology, for encouraging my interest in the *practical* side of product planning problems. I am indebted to Ken Herlingshaw, of Xerox Ltd, for his assistance with the preparation of the final draft. Finally I am most deeply in debt to my wife Ofra, who managed to help me over the final stages of preparing the book.

1 Introduction

THE IMPORTANCE OF PRODUCT PLANNING

Product line change – the process by which a firm alters the range of products or services[1] which it sells – is one of the most important kinds of business activity. A firm's product range is one of the key determinants of its profitability and sales. Changes in the product line can produce major changes in a firm's fortunes, while all other elements of the firm's marketing strategy depend crucially for their success on the characteristics of products sold by the firm. Product strategy therefore has a claim to be one of the most fundamental elements of marketing strategy.

The way in which a firm actually goes about making a product line change is obviously important. Because the process of launching a new product, modifying an existing one or withdrawing a product takes up (and may release) resources, some kind of planning must be involved if the product line change is to be accomplished smoothly and without risk to the overall success of the firm. Even if the firm decides to change its product line simply because certain resources have become available or (in the case of a product withdrawal) are in great demand elsewhere in the firm, other resources will be involved and their release or acquisition will have to be planned.

Although some kind of planning will always be taking place during the process of product line change, the quality of this planning will vary tremendously. Some firms simply guess, on the basis of minimal information, that there is a market for a certain product and that the costs of producing it can be more than recouped by the revenue likely to be achieved. They then arrange their resources to produce and market it, with little or no consideration of the impact of the product on their overall performance. Other firms, often those for whom product line change is a relatively frequent occurrence, are so organised that they are able to research rapidly and thoroughly the prospects for a product and the likely costs of producing it, come to a decision about its viability very quickly, and efficiently implement the decision.

Economists, marketing analysts and others have produced a variety of techniques and models (such as contribution analysis, product life cycle theory, non-metric multi-dimensional scaling, marginal costing procedures and discounted cash flow techniques) which can be applied in the analysis of product strategy. Sometimes firms simply do not take steps to avail themselves of the techniques appropriate to their position. Sometimes the techniques themselves have very severe limitations (although these may in practice be due to the fact that those analysts who put the techniques forward as ways of solving product planning problems do not adequately stress the problems involved, which results in a blind application of the techniques without much consideration of whether they are appropriate for the problem in hand). But perhaps the most crucial problem, which may lead firms to avoid altogether the use of the appropriate techniques (or to their misuse of them), derives from the interdependence between the many factors involved in the product planning analysis. To overcome this problem, the various aspects of product planning need to be closely integrated.

THE INTEGRATED APPROACH
If the interdependence of the factors involved in the product planning process is overlooked, several problems are likely to arise. To take a simple example, consider a procedure for choosing between product strategies that relies implicitly on a particular marketing policy (without the dependence between the two ever being made explicit). Such a procedure is unlikely (except by chance) to lead to a firm's aims being realised if that marketing policy is changed. In more detail, suppose that a firm makes decisions on new products by applying the following simple rule :

> Produce any product which will produce more than a given annual revenue and yield a given profit margin on sales.

This is a rule which is commonly used, in one form or another, in many firms in the U.K. It is evident that it can produce widely varying rates of return on capital on new products if the ratio of capital input to sales revenue varies widely between products.[2] It often happens that the ratio of capital to sales does remain fairly constant between the products of a firm, because the type of products that it produces and the kinds of technology it chooses to produce them ensure that capital costs and total costs are kept in a fairly constant proportion. If a standard profit margin is used in this case, then the rate of return on capital will be kept constant. But if a new method of marketing is used for a new product such that much heavier commitments of capital are required (e.g. if a larger initial promotional effort is required) then the rate of return on capital will fall. If the target rate of return has been fixed by the firm on the basis of an assumed ratio of sales to capital, then this target rate of return will not be reached.

Of course this example begs a large number of questions. A more intensive promotional policy might increase sales relative to other overhead costs, compared with the average product already being produced by the firm. The overheads of the firm would therefore be easier to carry and the ratio of cost to price (excluding promotional costs) would fall. There are many other consequences of a change in promotional policy that the firm would need to investigate before it could work out the end result of the change. But it should by now be recognised that the basic problem with which the firm is faced is that of the interdependence of policies. If one factor is changed, the effect on the whole system is not normally self-evident.

When a product line change is made, several policy variables (e.g. pricing, promotion, distribution and production) are usually operated upon at once. This means that the problem of assessing the end result of the policy change is made that much more difficult to solve. The only way to resolve the problem is to investigate in detail the various areas of analysis. In the above example, for instance, the effect of different ways of marketing the new product on all cost components and on profits and sales would need to be investigated. It is certain that this investigation will not be localised, since normally other products produced by the firm will be affected.

It is easy to advise firms to attempt to integrate their product planning analysis. It is far more difficult to provide the firm with an adequate framework for doing so. That is the intention of this book. We take as the starting point of the analysis an investigation of company aims, for as long as the aims of the company are not made explicit there is no hope of producing a rational framework. From the clarification of the nature and status of company aims, the product planning framework evolves. However, before discussing company aims, the scope of this book needs to be clarified.

SCOPE OF THE APPROACH

Product planning is basically an element of corporate planning, though much of what is involved in product planning also occurs in the context of day-to-day management. Any planning activities in business share certain common characteristics. These could be called the logic of the planning process and in this book we try to draw out the common elements of this kind. With the recognition that, for marketing purposes, the physical characteristics of the product cannot be divorced from the many other variables in the buying situation, product planning has become less and less distinguishable from marketing planning, which is defined as the planning of all the variables that the firm can operate upon that determine how it presents itself to the markets in which it operates as a seller. The principal way in which product planning distinguishes itself from other elements of marketing planning is through the relative inflexibility of the variables involved in product planning. For example, a firm involved in the manufacture of domestic appliances can relatively easily change its pricing or promotional strategies, but cannot as easily change the design of its products. However, this distinction based upon the ease with which variables can be changed is not a cast-iron one. Minor modifications to design may be much easier for some firms to make than changes in distributional strategy. We cannot rely on definitions of product planning that suggest that the only concern is with the determination of the physical specification of products, since this would exclude consideration of many aspects of the product strategies of firms in the service industries which come legitimately under the heading of product planning. The definition of product planning therefore has to be left relatively open. It is left to the individual manager or student of management to decide whether the points covered by this book apply to the case under consideration.

The research on which this book was based was carried out in the United Kingdom in 1969–75. Studies were made of the product strategies of thirty firms in the packaging, grocery food, confectionery, electrical domestic appliance, commercial vehicle, office equipment and banking industries. The research produced a large number of cases in product planning. Because of the caution which nearly all the firms displayed in revealing any data in the area of corporate planning, the information gathered varied greatly in quantity and quality. For this reason, no attempt was made to quantify the results in any way, since any conclusions would have been highly unreliable. Instead, each case was analysed in depth as far as the data would permit. The interviews were carried out on a confidential basis. Therefore the origin of certain conclusions has been disguised.

The research was spread over several industries in order to cover variations in some of the major dimensions of analysis. For example, among the industries covered were some that produced durables, some that produced non-durables and some that produced services. Firms were selling to various levels of distribution (including direct to the consumer). The firms also had varying strengths of ties with firms abroad (which proved to be very important in some cases), and their products were of varying degrees of exportability. They varied in size from the very largest combine through to small independent firms and small subsidiaries of firms abroad. As we shall see, some of these factors can be crucially important.

The plan of this book is explained at the end of the next chapter, after we have discussed the logic of product planning and its relation to business aims. But before beginning this detailed consideration of product planning, some qualifications concerning the style of the book need to be made.

This book does not aim to present a highly detailed schema for the firm engaged in the process of product planning.[3] If it were to do this it would have to assume an availability of data which firms on the whole do not possess and are unable to afford. This book concentrates on the logic of the product planning process and on the status of the various moves that a firm can make in the product planning process. Above all, it is not a 'How to do it and do it well' book, since it is held that a firm can only decide for itself whether or not a detailed approach is suitable for its own purposes. If this book succeeds in making the practising manager and the student of management think more deeply about the product planning process, such that he is able to avoid the more common pitfalls involved, then it will have done its work.

2 Business Aims and the Logic of Product Planning

BUSINESS AIMS

In recent years, there has been considerable discussion of what the aims of the firm should be and of what they actually are, in both the literature of economists and that of management. There is not the space here to review this discussion in great detail,[1] but we do need to pay some attention to the more important points that have been raised in the discussion.

The view that is conventional to much business analysis is that firms should aim to maximise their profits. The fact that the profits concerned consist of a flow arising over time is taken into account by the suggestion that future profits be discounted by a suitable rate of interest. There is some argument about what value this rate of interest should take, but it is normally agreed that it be equal to the best rate that the firm could earn with its funds over the period in question, which is known as the *opportunity cost of capital*. Thus an amount of profit P occurring in year T is said to be worth the same as $P(1+R)$ in year $T+1$, where R is the rate of interest, because if P is not consumed in year T, it can be transformed into $P(1+R)$ by investing it for a year.

This simple discounting approach to profit aims is unsatisfactory because it is not correct to assume that a firm's preference for the distribution of profits over time will always be determined solely by the yield on investments. A firm can usually obtain different rates of return on its funds according to the degree of risk involved in each investment. Risk is not usually sufficiently quantifiable for an accurate expected value of the rate of return to be calculated.[2] Nor is it necessarily the case that all firms will have the same attitude to risk, such that an expected value is the appropriate measure, since firms may be either risk avoiders or risk accepters. Whatever the case, subjective estimates of risk will normally have to be used and this leads to an additional source of vagueness in the definition of profit maximising. Even if the best obtainable yield is on an investment within the firm, there will be little certainty about the probability distribution of the expected yield. Many of these points of course apply to any decision method, but most apply more strongly to the idea of profit maximising.

However, a more important objection to the simple discounted profit maximising approach to business aims derives from the uses to which profit may actually be put when it arises. A simple possibility is that it will be used to reduce borrowing needs (e.g. as a source of further investment funds), in which case the rate of interest *paid* on borrowed funds might be the most appropriate one to use rather than the rate of interest *received* on alternative investments. Whether these two rates are equal or not will depend partly on the perceptions of the lender concerning the riskiness of lending to the firm. There will also be differences associated with the structure of the capital market and the administrative costs of lending and borrowing. But leaving these considerations aside, at the time when the firm makes a new product investment it may not have any clear idea about the use to which future profits will be put except in the most general strategic terms. There will be several different claims on profits in the future, one of the most important of which is the claim of the shareholder. Here the question which the firm needs to consider is : how much more is it worth to the firm to be able to pay a given amount to shareholders in any particular year rather than in the following year? This question will not be answerable by reference simply to the likely future level of interest rates, since there may be some form of credit rationing (due to imperfections in the capital market or to government intervention) which prevents recourse to the capital market at the going interest rate. It may also be true that the firm will be in a particularly good or bad position at the time when these profits arise, and this will alter the rate of interest at which the firm can borrow. If the profit is likely to arise at a time when the firm's situation would otherwise be extremely difficult, then the profits will be worth more than if the same monetary amount became available at some other time.

It is clear that the dividend decision is crucial to the whole question of profit aims. Lintner[3] found that the process by which the dividend was decided tended to start with a consideration of whether the dividend rate should be altered at all. If management decided that this was definitely desirable, the level of current *net* earnings was the main influence on the amount of dividend alteration. Managers in most firms believe that shareholders have some right to profits, though this belief may be a rationalisation of fears of the consequences of low-dividend policies. This is a key point in the analysis. If paying a low dividend leads to the possibility that managers may lose control of the firm, then profits which enable reasonable dividends to be paid will be more valuable than profits in excess of the required amount. So the relative valuation of profits in successive years will depend on whether there is an anticipated trough in profits, whether the profits from the new product project will be large enough to make a significant difference to the size of the anticipated trough and on whether accumulated reserves (if any) will be large enough to carry the firm through the trough. If, on the other hand, managers are reasonably certain that overall profits in the future will be large enough to allow satisfactory dividends to be distributed, then all that needs to be taken into account is the effect of the profits on the internal cash flow of the firm and the managers' aims with regard to this cash flow.

Having looked at the question of the distribution of profits over time, we now need to examine the idea of maximisation. Technically, maximisation means making the best choice out of *all possible* courses of action. On the whole, it is now accepted that the idea of maximisation interpreted in this way is not very useful for the analysis of strategic decisions (which include product planning decisions). The resources absorbed by searching for and researching the various strategic possibilities and the delay imposed by the search means that firms have to limit their searches to only a few possibilities. To explain why a firm has not looked further for possible strategies, we need to make use of some kind of *satisficing* notion.[4] The term 'satisficing' describes a search procedure which ends when the firm finds a strategy which seems likely to yield a satisfactory performance (however this is defined) or when it finds several strategies of this performance level, in which case the firm then proceeds to choose between them.

The notion of satisficing can of course apply to any business aim, although usually its use is confined to profits and sales. One of its important qualities, for theoretical purposes, is that satisficing is less likely to lead to a conflict of aims. If two aims are being pursued by a firm, such as profits and sales, it is highly unlikely that the policy which leads to the maximising of the value of one of the variables (say profits) will also lead to the maximising of the other variable. Indeed, very often, the aims may be directly contradictory. In this example, it is obvious that sales can be achieved at the expense of profits in certain demand conditions just by reducing the price of a product or increasing promotional expenditure. With satisficing, the likelihood of this conflict occurring is much reduced. Once the profit aims of the firm are seen to be achievable by pursuing a particular new product project, the firm can also ensure that some attention is paid to the sales aspect. Of course, whether this can in practice be realised depends upon the aspiration levels of the managers involved. Aspiration levels are the levels of performance for the firm to which managers aspire, and it is these aspiration levels which partly determine the satisficing levels of the variables incorporated in the firm's aims. If the managers' aspiration levels for profits are extremely high, then the search procedure for new product possibilities may effectively approximate to a maximising procedure. This of course depends upon the level of managers' aspirations relative to the real possibilities that are open to the firm.

Given the points discussed above, we obviously need to be very careful in any discussion of profit aims. The problem is further complicated when we introduce other business aims, as in the foregoing analysis of satisficing. Several other factors will normally enter into the business aims that are involved in a product planning decision. These include sales levels, capacity utilisation, employment and liquidity. Furthermore, each component of the business aims of a firm can be interpreted in several ways. For example, profit aims may be in the form of absolute levels of pre-tax or post-tax profit, rate of return on capital, rate of return on sales and so on. Sales aims may be expressed in terms of absolute levels, rates of growth over time, market share for the different markets in which the firm operates and so on. Capacity utilisation aims may be fixed at different levels for different plants. Where employment aims are concerned, there may be different aims applied to different groups of workers (e.g. skilled, unskilled, managers and sometimes groups of workers of varying status who are regarded as key workers), while the proportion of the work force on full-time working may be important, as may be the growth or shrinkage of the total work force.

As mentioned before, these aims may be and usually are in conflict with each other. We are forced to assume in this book that firms have some way, however formal or informal, of resolving conflicts of aims. This does not mean that all firms are assumed to end up with one clearly defined aim, but simply that their aims are explicit enough for product planning analysis to be applied to them. This entails that the rate of trade-off between aims be made explicit. For example, managers making a product planning decision need to know, at all stages of the analysis, but especially at the search stage, how much priority the firm wishes to give to profit and how much to sales. If the trade-off between aims is not made explicit, then there will be all sorts of problems involved in applying almost any business analysis, but that is not taken to be the concern of this book.

It may of course be the case that some aims coincide in practice, especially when we take the time dimension into account. For example, behaviour that appears in the shorter run to be sales-orientated might in fact be a result of longer run pursuit of profits.[5] In this case, present profits might be sacrificed for future profits by following a low-price policy which secures a large market share. Equivalence of aims may occur because of the firm's own policy. For example, adherence to a particular profit/sales ratio as a matter of policy makes absolute profit aims and absolute sales aims effectively equivalent if the policy is rigidly adhered to, since an increase in sales is automatically accompanied by an increase in profits. However, circumstances are rarely predictable enough for a firm to be able to adhere rigidly to a policy of this kind. There will therefore normally be some conflict of aims within a firm, and its existence and possible consequences need to be borne in mind throughout the analysis. It may be that the firm delegates decisions in such a way that only managers at the highest level are faced with the problem of resolving this conflict. This might be done by instructing lower level managers to follow one aim only. However, this does not remove the problem for the firm, but merely shifts its location.[6]

AIMS AND STRATEGIC CONSTRAINTS

The idea of a business aim is very closely related to that of a self-imposed constraint. If managers hold that their firm should produce only one kind of product, for example, this view effectively constitutes the introduction of a further business aim, namely that the firm aims to produce only this kind of product. One of the most common self-imposed constraints found in the firms of the developed world is based upon the idea that a firm's strategy is optimally decided upon on the basis of the characteristics of the resources it currently owns or has the use of. This constraint is also one to which many writers on strategic issues subscribe. The approach is implicit in texts on strategic decisions of all kinds which suggest that the first step in the process of strategy change should be to compile an inventory of the resources, skills and other capabilities of the firm to give an indication of the possibilities that are open to it.[7] This simple view of strategic evaluation is not accepted in this book. Nor is another simple view which is very similar to this resource-based view, namely that policy is normally best directed to satisfying the demands of a certain set of customers (as exemplified by the statement – often found in company reports – that a particular firm is in the business of supplying the needs of a certain kind of customer). We first consider the resource-orientated view of strategic evaluation.

In principle at least, the current set of resources owned or controlled by the firm is relevant only in that it determines the degree of difficulty that might be associated with a move to another set of resources that would be needed to produce a certain kind of new product. In the real world, very few resources are completely unobtainable in the long run. It is rather the cost of obtaining them (this includes the cost of delays) and the effect of this cost on cash flows in producing a divergence between desired and actual positions that makes present resources important. Let us consider in more detail one of the most important resources used by the firm, namely management resources.

Suppose that a firm is earning a high rate of return (relative to managers' expectations) on its existing product range and that it is considering how to change its policy in accordance with its aims, which include real growth of sales and profits. It may regard the fact that its marketing staff are currently stretched to their limits (as far as time and ability are concerned) as an indication that it should expand by acquisition rather than by acquiring marketing staff and other resources separately. There is often a tendency, even for strategic purposes, to regard middle and especially higher management as an overriding constraint, despite the fact that an increase in staff recruitment might provide more opportunities for relocation of management according to proven abilities. Just because certain managers have specialised in dealing with a certain kind of product or market over a period of time, this does not mean that they are the best qualified to deal with those products or markets. This is effectively a blind spot in strategic decision-making, and can occur with respect to other resources as well.

However, there are *real* limitations imposed by the current resources of the firm. The way in which they impinge on the principles of product planning is not simple. It depends upon whether 'product planning' is taken to include diversification by merger as well as the normal process of internal evolution of new products. If there is a real possibility of acquiring suitable new products by taking over or merging with other firms, then the principal resource constraints are financial (can the firm afford to purchase enough of the equity of another firm with appropriate products to gain control, given the possibility of offering its own stock as a medium of purchase?) and managerial (does the firm possess or can it obtain the necessary managerial resources to achieve the integration of the newly acquired firm into the management system already in existence?). But if the product line change is to be achieved solely with the use of the internal resources of the firm together with resources purchased separately on the open market, then the effect of resource constraints will be quite different.

One of the most important reasons for accepting resource constraints as crucial lies in the existence of uncertainty concerning the consequences of any changes that the firm might make. Suppose that a particular firm has in the last few years achieved on its new product investments (assuming that it is able to calculate the return separately) a return on capital that is substantially higher than its average rate of return on capital. Suppose too that there is no real problem in obtaining manufacturing capacity or technical research capacity or any of the appropriate material or labour inputs required for further developments at a cost that would enable the firm to achieve its required profit levels. The firm, we assume, finds that the principal limit to the rate at which it can launch new products lies in the capacity of marketing staff to handle them. Why then might not the firm simply hire more marketing staff to enable it to accelerate its rate of new product introduction?

The first reason is that the firm cannot be sure that the changes in its organisation produced by the introduction of new staff will not restrict its ability to produce successful new products. A firm may not be certain why it has been successful in the past, even if it has been very successful. It may easily ascribe its success to the wrong factor. For example, the firm may have a strong market position (in the sense that competition is weak) which accounts for the success of its products, but it might ascribe the success of its products to careful market research and well thought-out marketing strategies. The firm may have some idea that the success of its products is also in some way related to the standard of competition, but it may not be sure of the extent of the relation. If this is the case, it will be aware that it is difficult to estimate the effects of a change in the size or the structure of its marketing organisation on its new product successes. It will also have to bear in mind the effects of any expansion of its marketing staff on the management of its existing products.

Uncertainty about the accuracy of its judgements concerning the reasons for success may lead the firm to be cautious about expanding its purchases of a scarce resource because it is not sure about the effects of the expansion upon its performance. There is, however, a second important area of uncertainty that can affect the firm's decision. A firm cannot be fundamentally sure that good profit rates on existing products indicate the likelihood of good profit rates on new products, even if they are introduced in the same market area. Economists and management writers often take the view that high profitability in an activity is a signal that more resources should be allocated to that activity.[8] This is based upon the technical assumption that the relationhip between profits and investment is a continuous one and that investment is undertaken in small enough units such that the relationship between return and investment does not fall. In economists' language, the marginal rate of return on investment may be falling, but the slope of the curve describing the marginal rate of return may not be steep enough for small increases in the amount of investment to display a falling rate of return. This situation is described in Fig. 2.1.

If the profitability function is defined as the relationship between the measure of profit and the capital input, then a continuous function

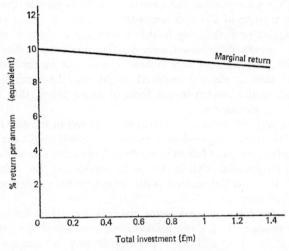

FIG. 2.1 Return on investment (I)

would appear as in Fig. 2.1. For the rate of return not to decline substantially with further investment, the next investment must be very small as measured on the horizontal axis. However, the function might be similar to the one depicted in Fig. 2.2, in which case there would be a very significant decline with further investment at the point of discontinuity. Such a discontinuity might be caused by a change in the

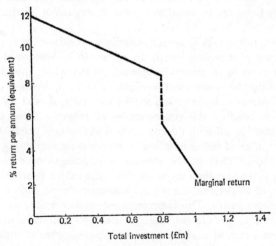

FIG. 2.2 Return on investment (II)

nature of the opportunities open to the firm. For example, there might have been a spate of technical innovations all of which are at present fully exploited, such that any further investment could not rely on the advantage previously possessed over existing products. A discontinuity might also exist because any further investment in the markets in which the firm is already involved might provoke retaliation from other firms in the market in the form of lower prices, thus reducing the return on investment.

Another possible source of a relatively large fall in the rate of return on a new product compared with existing products might derive from the fact that investment has to be made in large units due to the nature of capital equipment. This is termed by economists 'the indivisibility of inputs'. In many industries it is simply not possible to consider small additions to plant.

Put in more common-sense terms, the fact that a firm has succeeded with new products in a given market area beforehand does not necessarily imply that it will have the opportunity of making equally successful investments in the same market area in the future. The underlying conditions of a stable relationship between investment and profitability are unlikely to exist.

The conclusion of this argument is that unless the firm has very good reason to believe in the constancy of returns to any given resource (whether it be marketing management or new product investment), it will normally be uncertain about the outcome of a major change in its pattern of resource allocation. This uncertainty is likely to arise particularly strongly in relation to management resources and it explains why firms try to avoid too rapid an expansion in the use of this resource.

However, to explain is not necessarily to condone. It is easy to fall into the trap of excusing inertia by reference to 'uncertainty'. This is where the need for a rational approach to the whole question of product planning becomes most evident. The firm, instead of treating certain resources as more or less fixed constraints, should try to analyse as far as is possible the consequences of relaxing those constraints. Intead of starting off with the *condition* that any new product produced must be capable of being handled by the existing marketing team, say, the firm should look at the overall consequences of expanding the marketing team and then try to establish the extent to which satisfying various types of demand causes the consequences of such a relaxation of constraints to vary. This is because the resources that the firm needs in order to satisfy different kinds of demand will vary according to the type of demand and because the consequences of relaxing constraints of the kind discussed depend on the precise direction in which the constraints are relaxed. If a firm finds that it is incapable of planning without using some kind of relatively arbitrary resource constraints, it should at least periodically inspect some of the policy options that these constraints preclude the firm from pursuing and try to establish whether some relaxation of the constraints is worth while. Obviously, the cost of acquiring information on the consequences of the various kinds of policy changes made possible by the relaxation of constraints will be a crucial factor in determining the extent to which a firm can keep these constraints under review.

Having considered some of the problems inherent in the resource-constrained approach to product strategy, we now need to consider the related approach which considers the type of customer or market to which the firm is currently selling to be a crucial constraint, i.e. the market-constrained approach.

This approach is used very extensively in industry. Statements in company reports and by managers to the effect that the firm is in a particular line of business (e.g. the transport business) are ample evidence that this type of view of strategy is fairly common. The importance of this type of statement should not be exaggerated, however. Firms which subscribe to such statements often adopt fairly broad definitions of the defining terms in the statements. All the same, such statements still indicate an *a priori* restriction on the firm's product strategy. Sometimes it is even more restrictive than the resource limitation because it effectively combines a resource limitation with it. A firm's managers might argue that the firm's resources give it a comparative advantage (compared with some typical or average firm) in dealing with a particular market and that therefore the firm should not seek to make some fundamental change either in the type of resources that it uses or in the type of market in which it sells. This fixed market restriction is rejected as an *a priori* restriction for the same reason that the resource-orientated approach is rejected as an *a priori* restriction, i.e. because it rules out (or may rule out) possibilities which are more likely to yield good results as defined by the aims of the firm. In fact resource- or market-constrained approaches can in certain circumstances yield definitely bad results. A firm may identify its strength as lying in its marketing management and look for demand areas where success requires a very high marketing input and find, once it is involved in the new market, that the type of marketing ability required for success in the new market is completely different from the ability that it possesses. In such a case, a more open-ended approach to the employment of resources might have yielded a better result. Similarly, a firm which defines its business by the market in which it operates may embark on the production of a product which it has not designed very carefully because it did not consider seriously enough the use of consumption technologies derived from other markets.

Given this rejection of both the market-orientated and the resource-orientated constraints as *a priori* restrictions on product planning, the next stage of the analysis is to set out an idealised approach to product planning which facilitates the investigation of the extent to which constraints imposed *a priori* are really necessary and of the consequences of these constraints. The schema for this approach is presented in the following series of stages.

Stage 1
Fix aims and constraints.

Stage 2
Find areas of demand which seem to offer potential for satisfying both aims and constraints.

Stage 3
Find products within these areas and establish their characteristics.

Stage 4
Establish whether product specifications satisfy the constraints.

Stage 5
Establish whether products which satisfy the constraints can also be made to satisfy the aims of the firm.

Stage 6
Select all those product possibilities which as a group give the best performance within the constraints.

Stage 7
Produce and market those products.
(Note that the ordering of Stages 4 and 5 rests on the assumption that constraints are more rigid than aims. If this is not the case then Stage 5 would be taken first.)

This idealised stage model is designed to make it easy to integrate the various kinds of analysis involved in product planning. The chapters of this book do not strictly follow the stages, but they do follow them in a general sense. The chapters are arranged to make for ease of understanding, while throughout the book the emphasis is on the extent to which any techniques discussed are applicable in practice in the kind of situations in which firms actually find themselves. We take care to avoid too detailed a discussion of some of the more statistical techniques, since the rightful place for such a discussion is in the appropriate journals and textbooks. Too great an obsession with detail can obscure the extent to which a given approach is useful in practice.

The plan of the rest of the book is as follows. In Chapter 3, the choice of demand area is considered (Stages 1, 2 and 3). This is followed by a chapter on the product life cycle, a major element of demand analysis (Chapter 4). In Chapter 5, costs (Stage 3) and constraints (Stages 1 and 4) are dealt with. In Chapter 6, we examine the logic of the way in which demand and cost analyses are brought together (Stages 5 and 6). In Chapter 7, some marketing and organisational aspects are brought together (Stage 7). In Chapter 8 we bring together the conclusions of the book by presenting a hypothetical case history demonstrating the approach and its problems.

3 Demand and Product Planning

INTRODUCTION

Demand analysis plays a central part in the process of product planning. In principle, a firm should be continuously reviewing the demand situation not just for its existing products but also for products it might want to produce. In practice of course the cost of collecting and processing information (a major component of which is the managerial time required to digest it) limits the search for information to those market areas in which the firm is currently involved. Even where research is as limited as this, it often consists of simply obtaining market research information on the current state of the market (especially in terms of market shares) without any attempt at forecasting likely developments in the market on different assumptions about consumer behaviour, income, technical developments and so on.

However, we are not so much concerned in this book with what firms currently do (except to the extent that this indicates the aims and constraints according to which they operate). We are concerned rather with how a firm which is considering the possibility of product line change can in practice arrive at an appropriate choice of demand area[1] which will encompass the product. It is recognised that the firm's information-gathering resources are limited, so it is suggested here that the firm's investigation of demand should go through at least two stages. The first of these stages is called here the *delimitation stage*, which means the stage at which the firm selects the area for intensive demand research. The second of the stages is called the *intensive stage*, which is, as it suggests, the stage of intensive demand research associated more or less strongly with particular product possibilities. There is no reason in principle why more than one stage should not be undertaken, but this minimal division of the process enables us to explore in an uncomplicated way the logic of a multiple-stage research process.

THE DELIMITATION OF THE AREA FOR INTENSIVE DEMAND RESEARCH

The fundamental questions to be answered in this section can be summarised in the following general composite question :

'In what areas of demand is there scope for the firm to produce new products and be at some kind of advantage (*vis-à-vis* other firms that are already involved in these areas or that are likely to become involved in them) which will help the firm to realise its aims, and in what areas of demand is no significant advantage over other firms necessary for the realisation of the firm's aims?'

Within this composite question, there is an implicit division. This division is between the analysis of overall demand in abstraction from the competitive situation and the analysis of demand when the structure of competition is taken into account. For example, a firm investigating the electrical domestic appliance market would be interested both in the trends in demand for each type of appliance and in the extent to which it would be possible, given the likely evolution of competitive structure in the market, to sell particular amounts of each appliance. It is of course true that these two aspects are not separate from each other. For example, the extent of a firm's interest in some overall market category will be determined by its views on the ease of entry into that market. On the other hand a firm is unlikely to want to launch a new product into a market for which the prospects in general are not good, except perhaps as a short-term expedient. In addition, it may consider it worth while entering a market in which competition is extremely intense because it considers the prospects good enough to justify the associated risk. Therefore the investigation of the overall demand position is a plausible prerequisite. In practice, of course, in investigating overall demand areas a firm will pay attention to what it knows of the competitive structure in each area.

THE ANALYSIS OF OVERALL DEMAND IN DIFFERENT MARKET AREAS

The first move at this stage is to establish the effect of constraints. It is accepted in this book that information problems force the firm to impose on itself some kind of general constraint on the type of product that it wishes to supply. For example, a firm manufacturing heavy commercial vehicles is unlikely to consider it worth while investigating the demand for confectionery, for even if the confectionery market did prove on investigation to be highly receptive to new products, the likelihood of the firm being able to obtain the required resources at a low enough cost is small. Yet genuine diversification which seems almost as extreme as this example

B

does take place, albeit in a usually random fashion, so when a firm does impose constraints of this kind on its search, it should realise that it may be precluding the pursuit of highly profitable opportunities. However, a firm cannot ever find out what the consequences of relaxing a constraint of this kind are without investigating in detail the demand area that the relaxation of the constraint opens up. At the same time it is unlikely to want to investigate a demand area outside its constrained area unless it has already decided to relax the constraint and put some investigative resources into a new area. So there is something of a vicious circle here, a circle which has been created by information problems and uncertainty. The circle can only be broken by a definite decision to break out of it, and this usually happens when the firm hits by chance on a new product possibility outside its own product area and decides to investigate the possibility of producing it. Leaving this possibility aside, however, we have to accept at this stage whatever constraints the firm adopts and be content with a summary of the reasons why firms adopt constraints of this kind and how these constraints can be relaxed. The following points summarise this briefly.

1. Most firms adopt resource constraints and/or market constraints because they feel that it would be too costly (either in terms of a low rate of return on investment or simply in terms of the complete unavailability of funds) to change their resource base or the pattern of their customers. Basically, a resource constraint derives from a subjective estimate of returns on investment.

2. Many of the constraints that firms adopt are highly realistic in the short term, in the sense that it really *would* be too costly to relax them.

3. In the long term, there are various ways of relaxing constraints in a relatively uncostly way. For example, firms contemplating involvement in areas radically different from their current involvements may be able to obtain institutional co-operation (from research associations, Governments, suppliers, similar firms at home or abroad, distributors and so on) which enables the firm to make the change of resource base or market more easily than otherwise.[2] It is common for a firm making a radical change of this kind to have some assistance from an outside agency. The firm may have the resources to purchase a small (or even a large) firm operating in the desired area. In this case the transfer of expertise is made that much more easy. One of the commonest ways in which firms do diversify in this way is to seek firms overseas (in the United Kingdom, American partners are particularly widely used) which are trying to enter the home market and to make some co-operative agreement. Whatever the method used, the longer term the

change in product strategy, the greater the flexibility the firm can allow itself in relaxing constraints.

Even given the acceptance of some constraints of this kind, the analysis of overall demand is still left with a very broad area to cover. Obviously a firm cannot analyse all the demand within its constrained area, and some convenient device has to be designed to resolve this problem. Here, we resort to a combination of a satisficing process and a continuous search process. The meaning of this is made clear in the following paragraphs.

The essence of any satisficing process is that the firm should have a clear idea of what level of performance will render a policy or a decision acceptable to it. There must be some criterion of whether a given possibility should be admitted to the next stage of policy or analysis. Yet in the initial analysis of demand there will be no necessary relation between a given overall demand situation and the extent to which a firm's aims are realised. This is because the competitive and cost characteristics of the products which would satisfy demand in this area would need to be established before any acceptability criterion could be used, and these characteristics cannot usually be decided until a much later stage. However, there are certain criteria which are likely to lead to more successful products being launched, and the firm is forced to adopt criteria which are *probably* only suitable because without them the planning process can make no further progress. Hence for example the idea that 'growth' markets are *a priori* more suitable areas in which to launch new products than markets which are static.

In trying to establish what criteria are appropriate determinants of the acceptance of any particular demand area as being worth further investigation, it is recognised that any criterion could exclude possibilities which in fact have a very high potential. So we have to state beforehand that we are interested in criteria which are *probably* suitable for each individual firm. Once a criterion is adopted, however, the number of possibilities that satisfy it and that can feasibly be investigated by the firm will be determined by the search resources that it possesses (both financial and managerial). This number will also depend upon the speed with which the firm needs the investigation to be carried out. Obviously the constraints of both search resources and speed are arbitrarily imposed. Search resources can be acquired, but their productivity and hence the wisdom of acquiring them cannot easily be established until after the event. Nor can the wisdom of carrying out research with particular speed. For it may be that spending more than is currently being spent or taking time over the investigation will more than repay the firm. However, for the time being we have to accept this limitation.

The continuity of the search process is important because it means that even if some possibilities which might have yielded good results are excluded during the search process in one particular time period, they can still be considered in the search process in the following time periods. Although the nature of the possibilities may have changed and some may have disappeared entirely, it does mean that a relatively arbitrary criterion adopted for the satisficing search process may not exclude too many good opportunities.[3]

We now consider the nature of the actual criteria adopted. As was pointed out above, the criteria will be related to the aims of the firm. For the purposes of this book, the assumption is made that the firm's long-term aim is survival and that survival is best assured by the firm's involvement in markets which are not declining in real terms.[4] Within this, there is obviously still a wide range of possibilities, so the area is further delimited by the assumption of a preference for demand areas that are growing relative to the economy as a whole. Implicit in this is the assumption that firms prefer to maintain their importance in terms of size relative to the economy. But the fact that these particular criteria are suggested here does not make all other criteria invalid, nor does it preclude the rest of the analysis being useful if other criteria are adopted.

We now summarise briefly some of the techniques that may be useful for the analysis of overall demand in the product planning situation. There is a vast literature on demand forecasting in the fields of economics, marketing and operations research, and, as stated in the previous chapter, it is not the intention of this book to devote too much attention to the detail of techniques. We are more concerned here with the sequence in which the techniques are used and the logic of it.

The obvious way to start the analysis is first to consider the most general level of forecasting and then to progress to the particular.[5]

Any firm considering the introduction of a new product needs to consider the trends in overall economic activity. Even if the firm is principally concerned with its relative position in the markets in which it already operates, the overall trend will influence the characteristics of demand for particular types of goods (income changes will lead to changes in preferences). Forecasts at this very general level are usually obtainable from public sources (such as governments, consulting institutions and sometimes international bodies), but because the forecasting methods used by the institutions are not infallible, the practising manager and the student of management need to know something of the methodology on which the forecasts may be based and of the problems which may be produced by these methodologies.

If we take an assumed rate of growth of national income, we need to be able to establish what shares of this are taken by consumption (in the case of producers of consumer goods and services) and investment (in the case of producers of industrial goods and services).[6] Although the proportion of national income spent on consumption tends to be constant (leaving out the effect of taxation), there are circumstances in which this constancy may not hold, and this can lead to major changes in the markets for many goods. Therefore it is most important to establish how consumers' attitudes to their income are likely to change over the longer term as they become richer or (less frequently) poorer. In an age of inflation, it is also important to establish what kind of effect rapid overall changes in the price level have on the *real* consumption of consumers. There are all sorts of possible effects, depending on the extent to which the consumer is accustomed to inflation, ranging from an increase in saving because inflation is taken as a sign that worse times are coming, to an increase in consumption expenditure as consumers realise that it is relatively useless to maintain assets in anything resembling money. In the latter case, a considerable pay-off can accrue to the firm which estimates correctly the type of durable good that consumers are likely to move into. If the level of real national income is fluctuating, then it may be worth while trying to establish consumers' attitudes to their income, part of which may be considered to be permanent and part of which may be considered to be transitory. Spending out of these different parts of income may differ considerably in its pattern. There may also be good reasons for considering changes in the age structure of the population, since peoples' consumption patterns differ over their life cycles.

For the firm, these points serve as *caveats* against assuming a simple relation between consumption and income. Very few firms are actually able to analyse demand at such a general level, but they should all at least be aware that consumption forecasting is not a straightforward process and that the implications of changes in the overall level of consumption can be very diverse.

We have mentioned the relation between consumption and income, but it should be pointed out that income is not the only determinant of aggregate consumption, although in the long run it is the most important. Certain other determinants of consumption should be mentioned. One of the most important of these for short-term purposes is consumer liquidity. Especially in an age of inflation, when the rate at which prices and incomes are rising can get out of step, leading to sudden increases or decreases in consumer cash balances, the unloading of accumulated cash balances can cause large changes in the level of consumption. Timing the introduction of new products to correspond with such changes can be crucial in determining the success or failure of a product. In the United Kingdom and in the economies of certain other countries in which credit variables are used by the government as a means of controlling the level of national activity, managers have to be aware of the extent to which changes in credit variables are likely to occur and of the extent to which these changes are likely to affect the demand for goods which they are producing or considering producing.

These and other variables are the subject of intense investigation by economists and others, such that projections of greater or lesser accuracy of most of the relevant variables are usually available from some source or other. It should be noted, from a theoretical point of view, that even if a firm does not feel it needs to have a forecast of the overall level of economic activity in order to establish which areas of demand are most suitable for further investigation, if the firm's aim is to maintain its relative importance within the economy, then it needs to know how the national level of activity is likely to develop in order to establish its aspirations for the markets in which it will be involved. For this reason, knowledge of these variables will be useful to this kind of firm. Knowledge of these variables and the way in which they influence consumption will also help the firm to update any projections of consumption by itself.

The demand for investment goods is usually much more volatile than for consumer goods as a whole. This applies whether the goods are durable (e.g. fixed plant and equipment) or non-durable (stocks of inputs to be used up in the process of manufacture). Investment goods are often bought with money which has a substantial opportunity cost, whether it is actually borrowed or not, so that a crucial determinant of demand can be the condition of the various capital markets. Another important influence on this demand is the expectation of the buying firms concerning their products. These expectations are usually based on current trends, but can in the short run be quite volatile. On the other hand, the necessity for businesses to plan ahead may mean that the demand for certain categories of investment goods is easily forecastable from buyers' intentions, since manufacturing plans may have already been based on the expected purchase of the investment good. Expectations can in the short run be self-fulfilling because of the employment-creating consequences of investment activity. One reason for the instability of investment goods demand is the deferrability of replacement (this applies to consumer durables as well). But at some stage the replacement has to occur, since there is a level of service which will not be tolerable to the manufacturer. Therefore replacement demand acts as a stabilising influence, and prediction of replacement booms can be a key factor in the success of a product and hence in the suitability of a market for the launch of a new product. We now turn to a discussion of how the importance of these various factors can be determined.

DEMAND FOR GENERAL PRODUCT CATEGORIES

There are several general classifications of products which are useful in analysing demand, some of which have already been mentioned. These classifications include the following : consumer/industrial, durable/non-durable, good/service, exportable/non-exportable. A secondary classi-fication, which might be useful in some markets, could be based on the extent of government involvement in the market, since this can lead to a considerably different purchasing pattern. The location of each demand area to be investigated within each of these dichotomies will sometimes affect the way in which a forecast of demand is arrived at. But before discussing this, some clarification of the meaning of the term 'product' or 'good' as used in this section is needed.

Products can be of varying levels of generality. For example, a par-ticular make of car can be classified either as a transport good, a road transport good, a car, a car of a particular size or performance category, or a car of its particular make. Analysis is possible at all these levels. The difference in the analysis at each level will be caused by the degree of substitutability with other products. For example, if we are analys-ing the demand for cars, we need to investigate variables connected with public transport, but if we are analysing the demand for a particular make of car, we also need to take into account variables connected with other makes of car.

One further qualifying point needs to be made. Demand does not equal sales. Forecasts of future demand based upon past sales levels can be unreliable if they fail to take into account any shortages of supply that occurred and that were not reflected in the values of other variables, such as price). However, sales data are often the only data that are available, especially at such a general level, so that there is really no option but to use them. There is a further point concerning sales data which needs to be made. Sales are determined by the pro-ducts which are on offer. Without the products there would be no sales. If no suitable products are offered (and this may be a matter of technical progress) then there will be no corresponding sales. Therefore demand forecasting needs to be accompanied by some notion of tech-nological forecasting.

There are several techniques for actually forecasting demand. The first assumption that is made by most of them is that demand can be predicted on the basis of past data. The relationship will normally be expressible as a demand function, in which the level of demand is expressed as a function of some of the following variables : price of the product, income of the consuming group, prices of other relevant goods, tastes, distributional factors, population of the consuming group and the current stock of the commodity held by buyers. Conventionally, at least in economics, the important variables are taken to be price and income, with stocks playing an important part in the case of durable goods. However, other methods of forecasting which use the passage of time as a surrogate variable for most of the others have been developed, and we shall be paying considerable attention to one of these (the product life cycle) in the next chapter. For the time being we concentrate on more conventional techniques.

The crucial questions in forecasting for management purposes are the following :

1. Can the relationship between the variables be established with any confidence at all?
2. Can the variables which determine demand themselves be forecast?

If the answer to either question is in the negative, then the forecasting procedure is worthless.

There are basically two different approaches to forecasting. One method is to seek to establish correlations with variables which are forecastable, even if there is no causal relationship derivable on theoretical grounds. One example of this is classical time series analysis, in which the final sales forecast is made on the basis of the assumption that whatever the determinants of sales, they are in some complex way related to time, so that sales can be successfully forecast as a function of time, even if this is a very complex function. Various ways of breaking down the relationship are suggested. One way is to try to establish whether there are known patterns over conventionally determined time periods (monthly, seasonal, annual) and whether underneath these variations a trend can be discerned. Any established patterns are then given mathematical expression. The disadvantage of this and other similar approaches is that it does not establish *likely causal* factors, so that if factors which may have caused these variations in the past change out of pattern, the forecast itself may go badly wrong. However, if the factors which turn out to be important in any other kind of analysis prove to be unforecastable, then this kind of approach may be the best feasible one.

The demand function proper, on the other hand, does claim to establish relationships which have some causal basis in theory. The methods usually used to estimate the demand function are based on standard regression techniques as used in statistics and their derivatives. The variables usually included are the ones mentioned. Once for all changes are introduced by the use of dummy variables to impart a shift to the relationship.[7] The logarithmic form is often used to make the relationship more computable, while lagging of variables may be introduced if considered appropriate. First difference data may also be used.

We now consider the forecasting problems posed by each variable.

Price of the good

At this general level, when we are investigating the broadest of market categories, price has a meaning only as an index, since the market area will normally have many different products of different designs, sizes, etc. in it. This problem may be overcome for the purposes of approximate forecasting (which is what concerns us here) by the use of the price of a sample of products. However, the forecasting of prices raises serious problems. Suppose that for the purposes of this section we are interested in a forecast for the following ten years. This assumption of a ten-year forecast is not an implausible one, although the planning period actually decided upon will depend upon the type of industry with which we are concerned. Obviously for a fashion good the period will be much shorter than for a major piece of capital equipment. The period will depend both on the expected life of the product and on the required planning period. A ten-year forecast of prices would involve an investigation of costs and competitive structures over this period. This would normally be possible only at a superficial level (the level of guesswork), unless (as for example with raw material prices and food prices) there was published information and forecasts for some of the major components of the required analysis. The firm would probably have to assume that present trends in relative prices would be maintained unless specific technological changes were anticipated. The actual nature of the relationship estimated could vary considerably over the period in question. In particular, the firm would need to be aware of any possible threshold price levels, which would result in a shift in the relationship as the price suddenly made the good available to a wider market (or unavailable, in the case of a real price rise). The extent to which the product is traded internationally will also affect the importance of prices and costs. For example, if the domestic market were affected by a cost change which did not apply to foreign producers, then the result could be a change in the relationship between domestically produced goods' prices and demand. The effect of taxation has also to be taken into account in forecasting the relationship between price and demand. If the good is heavily taxed, there is a greater likelihood of proportional price change as a result of tax changes. Responses to price changes may vary if these changes are induced solely by tax changes.

Price of substitutes and complements
Here the firm first needs to establish what other products have the most crucial influence on the demand for the products in the area of demand under consideration. The breadth of the definition of products will of course be important here, as mentioned earlier. This process will then face precisely the same difficulties as outlined for the forecasting for the price of the product itself. It should be mentioned here that the price of other goods is really an abbreviation for all the relevant characteristics of other goods, so that if there is any likely change in demand or supply conditions (e.g. promotional factors), the firm should take it into account.

Income of buyers
The relationship between income and demand is one of the most important relationships for our purposes because income (which incidentally is often used by economists as a partial surrogate for changes in tastes) can alter so greatly over the long run, and with large changes in income usually come substantial changes in preferences. In addition, even if preferences do not change significantly, the rise in income leads to a relaxation of the budget constraint of the buyer such that he is able to buy more of any good. The relation can also be quite a complex one. For example, a buyer may have a minimum threshold level of income below which he will not buy the product as well as a maximum threshold above which he will cease to buy the product or will at least cease to increase his rate of purchase. If the relationship is more simple, it may be captured by a simple logarithmic conversion, but for more complex relationships, guidance may need to be sought from the situation in higher income markets.

Income forecasts are usually available for consumers, but corporate income forecasts are less readily available. However, these are slightly less important, since it is arguable that purchases of industrial goods depend most heavily on purchases of consumer goods. However, the nature of the relationship between purchases of investment goods and purchases of consumer goods is extremely complex. Normally, there will be some kind of lagging in the relationship, but there will also be some influence through expectations of firms about future consumer purchases which may not be based on past consumer purchases.

Tastes

Tastes are of course related to income, but because of the social process by which tastes are changed (usually modelled as some kind of diffusion process) there will normally be some kind of relationship with time. However, in a growing economy, income will usually be strongly correlated with time, so the effect of income may be better represented by first difference data, with some other variable (perhaps time) being used as a surrogate for the influence of tastes, although this can raise problems of multi-collinearity in statistical analysis. In the U.K. forecasts of tastes are often made on the basis of developments in high-income economies, such as the U.S.

A major problem that occurs with the analysis of the relationship of tastes with demand is the effect of manufacturers' own policy on tastes. Clearly, the existence of products influences tastes towards those products. Therefore any forecast of tastes and of the relationship between tastes and demand should try to take into account this effect, since major upsets to demand forecasts can be produced by changes in tastes induced by manufacturers.

One further point needs to be made concerning tastes. The analysis of tastes is usually the most difficult but often the most fruitful for a manufacturer considering a change in product policy. The major problem, since tastes can rarely be measured directly, is that of finding some variable with which tastes do vary. For example, in forecasting the demand for new cars, an important variable, which reflects the tendency of people to live in certain kinds of surroundings and thus their need to use a car, is the level of urbanisation (the proportion of the population of an area that live in towns). Similar kinds of variable can be found for most general categories of product, and identifying such variables can pay good dividends.

Population

Population usually has a fairly straightforward influence on demand, although its rate of change and the associated change in the age structure of the population may affect certain goods more strongly than others. For example, goods in the housing market often show high sensitivity to the rate of household formation, which is correlated strongly with the age structure of the population.

The forecasting of population changes does not present too great a difficulty for the individual firm, since forecasts are usually available from government sources. Although the accuracy of these forecasts is often open to question, it is unlikely that the individual firm will be able to do much better than these sources.

Stocks

The level of stocks is usually thought of by economists as a variable which is only of importance in the short term. The level of stocks indicates two things, namely, the likely replacement demand (due to depreciation of the quality of units of the product held in stock) and the extent to which demand for holding stock is itself satisfied (since the holding of stocks, in the case of goods like cars, televisions, etc., is itself a source of satisfaction). Various more or less sophisticated ways of analysing the relationship between stocks and demand have been invented, but the most important point for the firm to grasp is the extent to which stocks are made obsolescent rather than the extent to which they wear out. In addition, the firm needs to investigate the consequence of the obsolescence of stock (how the fact that a given stock no longer provides the same amount of satisfaction is related in quantitative terms to the level of demand). This is a matter for the long-term investigation of tastes rather than for the short-term statistical analysis of stock level changes.

Distribution

The distributional influence on the demand for a general category of commodity, like the price of the commodity itself, is strongly influenced by supply factors. The most important point here is that the extent to which distributors are independent of manufacturers (in the sense of being an independent entity) varies greatly. In some markets, the manufacturers are effectively the distributors, so that there is no separate influence of distributional factors at this level. In other markets, where manufacturers sell their product to the final buyer through one or more levels of distributors (whose major function is to change the location and size of average purchase of the product), the size and coverage of distributional agencies will have an obvious influence on demand. For many kinds of goods, the development of the appropriate retail system has been the key to the take-off of the product, and although sometimes this development has been due to the promptings of the manufacturers themselves, in many cases the manufacturers have not had the resources to do this. Therefore, when considering the likely evolution of demand in a particular market category, the firm needs to take into account whether the needs of products are adequately catered for by the present structure of distribution and, if not, whether this has resulted in an effective holding back of demand and, further, whether there is likely to be any change in the structure of distribution which will change the effective demand for the product. The forecasting of changes in the structure of distribution presents immense problems, but the firm should at least attempt some kind of sensitivity analysis to allow for this factor.

The factors mentioned above cover only the most important factors that determine demand in general terms. But they should at least provide guidelines concerning the type of analysis the firm must undertake in order to get an adequate picture of the opportunities likely to be available at the most general level. It is recognised here that forecasts which involve this level of generality are not the kind of thing that most firms can undertake on a regular basis. However, forecasts of this type are usually of general enough interest to searching firms for agencies and consulting organisations to make some attempt at them in order to identify the growth areas in an economy, so that for some market areas these forecasts are already available, at a price. Even if the firm is attracted to the idea of making a simple extrapolation of past trends, it should at least take account of some of the points mentioned above.

The firm will not of course find it worthwhile to continue investigating demand areas *ad infinitum*. So we assume the rationality of a cut-off point in the investigation (its location depending upon the firm's search resources). Thus by now the firm is assumed to have obtained a cross-section of demand estimates for various markets and has available some overall forecast of the level of activity in its domestic economy (to which, by assumption, the aspirations of its managers are linked).

We have already assumed that the firm is interested only in growth markets (markets which are growing relative to the economy). This means that any market areas which are not forecast to expand relative to the economy will not be considered further. However, if it is assumed that the firm has to carry out all the forecasting by itself, then it is likely that some further cut-off rule will have to be used in order to limit search activity. It is arguable that the following kind of decision rule would be a reasonable one to use (although its interpretation leaves many questions unanswered) :

Allow through possibilities based on the use of several different resource bases.

The justification for such a decision rule is that it might turn out that markets which are currently growing fast will shortly run up against some resource limitation. At the same time, it might also be the case that markets which have not been growing very fast have had their

growth restricted by the lack of certain key resources. Average possibilities may also therefore turn out to run up against a resource limitation in the future, so a rule of this kind, which encourages the firm
not to accumulate too many possibilities which can only be provided
for through the use of a particular resource base, at least allows the firm
some flexibility in its operation in future periods.

The actual rate of growth of the demand area relative to the economy which serves as a cut-off point in the analysis is something that
cannot be determined beforehand. Nor can the number of demand
areas which the firm should admit to the stage of intensive demand research. Here, the analysis has a severe limitation.

In practice, the firm's preference among those areas which satisfy a
particular rate of growth criterion will be for those which can most
easily be satisfied by using resources that the firm already owns or has
the use of or which it thinks it can obtain easily, especially if it is
envisaging a rapid change in product policy (and here it is usually the
case that the firm cannot see its way to providing resources for the
very longest term research, such that most research is for immediate
possibilities). Even over the longer term, where resource constraints
are not so stringent, this will be the preference. However, even if the
resource constraint were accepted in a general way at this stage, it does
not always restrict the field of consideration very much, since many of
the firm's resources (especially financial ones) are quite flexible. At this
stage, all we can do is to assume that the firm will somehow make the
choice between two general types of strategy, the *risk-avoiding* strategy
and the *risk-accepting* strategy. The risk-avoidance strategy would involve accepting for the stage of intensive demand research the first few
areas investigated which exhibited the required growth rate and did
not involve any major departure from the existing resource structure
on the part of the firm. Risk acceptance would involve the firm's
accepting all demand areas for further investigation which had a very
high growth rate, irrespective of their resource demands.

THE STAGE OF INTENSIVE DEMAND RESEARCH

It is at the stage of intensive demand research that competitive structures need to be taken more formally into account. It may be that a
particular demand area is very promising whatever the likely evolution
of the competitive structure within it, but normally the firm will have to
take this structure into account. We therefore restate the question
which lies behind demand analysis in order to show where competitive
structure fits in, with the one restriction that the delimitation stage is
already assumed to have been carried out.

'In what areas of demand within the area delimited for intensive demand research is there scope for the firm to become involved and be at some kind of advantage (which will contribute to the realisation of the firm's aims) over firms that are already involved in these areas or likely to become involved?'

In answering this question, we arrive at a more exact understanding of whether it is important to use existing resources intensively and to service existing customers. But first we need to analyse the concept of advantage.

THE DEFINITION AND IMPORTANCE OF 'ADVANTAGE'

It needs to be understood first of all that the concept of advantage is not used here in a purely static sense. When a firm is said to have some advantage over another firm, this can be taken to include the situation in which it is *capable* of developing an advantage over its competitors. This is obviously not identical to its already possessing such an advantage, but the difference is principally one of the time scale of the comparison. If the firm already possesses some kind of advantage, then the costs and benefits of using it for policy purposes will obviously not be the same as where it is capable only of developing the advantage. This does present some serious difficulties with definitions. There may be some situations in which two firms are using exactly the same set of physical and financial resources and selling to the same set of customers, yet one of them can be considered to have the advantage over the other as far as servicing future developments in the market is concerned because it possesses certain information about technical or demand factors such that it could in principle better arrange resources to satisfy demand.

Advantage is a multi-dimensional concept. It covers at a minimum all the commercial activities of the firm, which can be characterised as follows :

> *Production activities*
> Machines used, raw materials (handling and using), workers' skills, technology, location of facilities, type of product produced (size, perishability, handling characteristics), design of product.
> *Purchasing activities*
> Raw materials, labour, management, finance, capital equipment, etc.
> *Selling activities*
> Type of customer (income, class, location, loyalty, sex, age, etc.).
> Type of order (size, location, frequency, timing, whether on credit, etc.).
> Type of outlet (size, location, type of organisation, etc.).

This characterisation is not exhaustive and some of the categories overlap, but it should serve as a fair basis for the firm to evaluate likely advantage. We now have to consider how advantage is actually defined for any particular category of activity. As we have stressed before, advantage is a relative concept, dependent as it is on the characteristics of the firm's actual or potential competitors. This is one of the reasons why approaches which suggest the matching of new products to resources, without stressing that resources are important only if the firm's *relative* endowment of them is strong, are unsatisfactory.

The extent to which a firm has an advantage in a particular market area can be evaluated only by a comprehensive examination of the characteristics of the firm and of its competitors. It should be noted that, for any given demand area, the most competitive firms will not necessarily be the same for each type of activity. One firm may be well placed to exploit a demand change through its production skills and another through its marketing involvement. The comparison between firms will in principle consist of an evaluation of all the individual characteristics (as detailed above) of firms who at first sight seem well placed to satisfy demand in the area under investigation. Here we face problems of procedure (how should the firm go about comparing advantages?) and of the extent of the investigation (how many firms should the firm considering the policy change investigate?).

This is a massive task, and the best that we can do here is to outline a way in which the firm might make a start on the problem. The following is suggested as an approach.

Assume that the firm we are assessing currently produces a product set defined as P by means of resource set A and sells to market set X. We abbreviate this by describing the firm as $A–P–X$. P is defined by the product-service combination of the firm. A is defined by all the resources used as outlined above in the characterisation of the activities of the firm. X is defined by the buying units (individuals, firms, etc.) to which the firm currently sells. Let us now make the assumption that the firm has already investigated various markets within the particular demand area in question, on the grounds that these markets are growing at an appropriate speed, which will depend on the firm's attitude to risk. Suppose the demand areas which the firm has investigated to be called D, E, F and G. Assume that D is the one in which the firm is already involved and in which many of the products are produced with the use of resources from the set A, the set which the firm already uses. D is also characterised by many products of the type P (which the firm is already producing) and many customers of the type X, to which the firm is already selling. We call this market D the *base market* of the firm. Suppose that the other demand areas are characterised by the resource, product and customer sets as indicated below :

Demand area	Resource set	Product set	Customer set
D	A	P	X
E	A	Q	Y
F	B	R	X
G	C	S	Z

The firm now has to assess the likelihood of other firms being able to assemble $A–Q–Y$, $B–R–X$ and $C–S–Z$ combinations respectively. If this has already happened, the firm has to assess how difficult it would be to sell products of the general types Q, R or S in the face of the established competition. This is partly a matter of establishing the nature of barriers to entry, both for the firm itself and for potential competitors, and of investigating how such barriers could be set up after the firm's entry. Where resource sets are concerned, the most important question concerns the general availability of resources to all firms and to the particular firm in question.

Suppose that resource set A is what could be called an engineering set (which in the context of this example means that the firm in question is already involved in engineering). There are very large numbers of firms in the U.K. involved in engineering, but the product (P or Q) will make these resources more specific. There is no short cut to finding out which other firms are most heavily involved in a particular product area. Sometimes the information will simply not be available, especially if firms are multi-product ones. But often informal sources of information will be able to give some kind of indication as to whether potential competitors actually do possess the resources needed for entry into a particular market.

Perhaps more important than finding out whether any other given firm has the resources which are likely to be needed for success in a given product/market area is the question of the *importance* of the resource/product base. In order to assess whether a potential competitor will hinder the chances of the firm's own success in a particular market area, the firm has to assess the relative importance of possessing different resources and operating from different market bases. The only way in which a firm could in principle do this is through a comparison of past moves of firms both within and outside their existing bases in the appropriate market area. Here, it is trying to find some answer to the question 'How difficult will it be to move from resource set A to resource set B or from customer set X to customer set Y and what will be the impact of this move on the success of the product?'

There is a tendency which is commonly found in industry which is difficult to guard against, namely the tendency in any analysis to stress the advantages which the firm possesses and to play down those categories of analysis where the firm cannot be shown to have any advantage.

If a firm establishes, from past strategies of other firms (and this is about the only information it has) that moves from one base to another are infeasible, then it must obviously restrict the area for future analysis. But if the feasibility of moves of base can be established, then the scope of the analysis shifts to the question of resource acquisition. Here the firm needs to consider carefully not the general problems of resource and market diversification, but the particular problems that firms diversifying from similar resource and market bases faced in the past, paying particular attention to the quality of management.

We now assume that, through the analysis of competitive structures, the firm has been able to choose a small number of market sets as suitable for analysis. It now has to establish, within the market area narrowly defined, what the exact demand conditions are for new products.

MICRO DEMAND ESTIMATION

The first problem that we face here is that the characteristics of the new product are not definitely fixed. At this stage the investigation is at the level of demand for a type of product rather than demand for a particular design of product. This is because the product itself has yet to be designed, and the design will be according to which type of product is found to be most promising from the demand and cost point of view.

There are two dimensions to the analysis of demand, the depth of demand and the breadth of it. Roughly speaking, the depth of demand is a question of how much a particular consumer whom we know to want a product of a particular type would be willing to pay for that product. The breadth of demand is a matter of how many consumers would be willing to pay, say, above a certain price. The reason why we have not used the simple demand curve analysis here is that we will be talking in terms of demand for characteristics rather than demand for products for some of the time. The depth of a want that is felt has a crucial impact on the price that a consumer is willing to pay for a product that satisfies a number of wants. The second reason for separating these two points is that it is easy to fall into the trap of assuming that in general a broadly felt want for a product indicates that the product is more likely to be successful than one which satisfies a deeply felt want for fewer people. In addition, a deeply felt want is likely to allow for more leeway when it comes to the evaluation of production costs.

In order to estimate what demand is likely to be in a given narrow product area, product characteristics have to be defined. These cannot be chosen arbitrarily, unless the firm has in mind the exploitation of a particular technical development. In principle, the firm first has to establish what characteristics are required by consumers in the market in question. It then has to establish whether there is any clustering of these wants or, in other words, whether particular bundles of characteristics are required by consumers such that a given characteristic is valued only if it is accompanied by another characteristic. For example, the speed of air flight might be valued by a consumer only if it is accompanied by a particular level of safety.

The general problem of establishing dimensions of analysis can be illustrated with reference to cars. A car has a number of characteristics, including seating capacity, speed, acceleration, strength of body and so forth. These are the dimensions of demand. The ones that were listed were fairly obvious ones. But there may be some dimensions which are not so obvious yet which may be important to many (potential) consumers of a product. These dimensions of analysis cannot always be established by armchair speculation. The best way of establishing the dimensions of demand is by in-depth interviewing of customers and potential customers. But it should be remembered that the product planning decision is a long-term one, so that there will always be problems of estimating how the dimensions of demand may change in their identity and in their relative importance. Where the market is a very newly developed one (and of course the firm may have in mind the development by itself of a new market) there will be a major problem as far as identifying the future consuming population is concerned. The same problem of future changes is also raised where the valuation of different characteristics is concerned.

There are various methods which have been used to establish the valuation of characteristics of products which may not yet be in production. One of the most interesting is the *abstract mode model* as used by Quandt and Baumol.[8] This model was designed for use in the field of transport products (hence the use of the term 'mode', which means a method of transport). The starting point of the analysis is a recognition that a given physical product will have different characteristics for the consumer in different market situations. Thus, between two nearby towns rail may be the fastest means of transport, while between two other towns which are more distant from each other, air may be the fastest mode. In the case of transport products, each mode between two towns would not be identified by its name. Instead, it would be identified by a list of its characteristics, such as speed, comfort and so forth. Baumol and Quandt hypothesise that demand for each mode will depend upon (*a*) the absolute performance level of the 'best' mode on each criterion and (*b*) the performance level of each mode on each criterion relative to the best mode. This is almost analogous to the determinants of overall market demand and the determinants of market share. In the case of transport, many of the variables are more easily measurable than for other products, in particular those of travel time over a given route and frequency of departure. Also, choice situations (which are crucial to any analysis of demand) are to some extent more easily identifiable. Thus Baumol and Quandt can talk about a network of arcs between nodes (identified here as population centres), each arc having different lengths and each mode having possibly different characteristics over each arc. But, in order to take account of non-quantifiable dimensions, such as comfort and danger, they have to assume that consumers are modally neutral. If people are, for example, averse to air travel (say because of a subjective estimate of danger), then a special dummy variable has to be introduced to shift the relationship. Using a simple example of two product characteristics, they suggest that an equation representing the function $T_k = f(H_b, C_b, H_{rk}, C_{rk}, N)$ can be fitted, where H_b and C_b are absolutely the best travel time and cost by any mode, H_{rk} and C_{rk} the relative travel time and cost for mode k, N the number of modes serving the arc and T_k the number of trips along an arc by mode k in the period of analysis. At this stage the modes are assumed to be of roughly equal size. Then, the characteristics of the equation are estimated from the modal choice statistics that are available from the network of arcs. Then, if a further mode is introduced over an arc of the network of routes, once its characteristics have been established, its share of the travel along that arc can be calculated using the coefficients that have been established by statistical manipulation. Of course, if the network is made more complex to allow for real-life variations in characteristics and if allowance is made for different size nodes, then variables have to be introduced to represent population, income in nodes, industrial character of nodes, etc. In addition, further characteristics of the transport products would have to be added (e.g. average waiting time for departure, which is a function of the distribution of arrival times, comfort, etc.).

As was pointed out above, this model is easier to apply in the transport product choice situation because of the importance of certain easily quantifiable variables in the choice and because of the relative ease of identifying choice situations (i.e. the need to travel from one node to another) and demand characteristics. Suppose, however, that we were considering a particular part of the confectionery market. First we would need to establish and measure the different dimensions of preference. For this, we would need to establish why the consumers in our sample had decided to buy confectionery at all, what had determined their choice in terms of general categories (price, sweetness, presentation, etc.) and then what the rate of trade-off between the various characteristics had been in the choice between the different products available. This would require far more work on the consumer psychology side than the abstract mode model suggests. However, the model does present the logic of one approach to the analysis of choice which will help the manager to organise his thoughts on the question. If the manager is trying to establish what dimensions of demand are likely to be crucial in determining the demand for a product, if he can separate several choice situations, he can at least proceed to formulate hypotheses about the reasons for particular choices on the basis of this model.

There has been other work in this area which can help the manager arrive at some indication of demand for characteristics.[9] One approach is that of Stefflre, who aimed to study the structure of various markets in order to find gaps in product preferences not adequately served by existing products.[10] His approach was as follows. First, in order to determine the boundaries of *product markets*, a small number of consumers (less than 50) are asked to judge whether each of a specified set of items (products and brands) is appropriate to each of a specified set of aims. Computer analysis determines (*a*) the judged similarity of each use to each other use in terms of whether the same products are seen as appropriate for the pair of uses and (*b*) the judged similarity of products in terms of their pattern of uses. These analyses are used to determine which items constitute the market of interest. This smaller set of items which are in general terms considered by consumers to have a particular set of uses, this set of uses in turn being judged to be similar, is then presented to another small heterogeneous sample of consumers who are asked to judge through rank ordering the similarity of each item to every other item. They are also asked to suggest features or ways in which items so judged are similar to each other. Techniques of non-metric multi-dimensional scaling are then used to find configurations of products in an *n*-dimensional space which affords the greatest consistency with the judged-similarity measures. If this statement is explained in simple two-dimensional terms, all that it means is that we have a map of two characteristics of products and we try to place products such that those judged to be similar with respect to each characteristic will be at the same level on the map (or at least approximately the same level), while those judged to be different are not. This is a simple process in two dimensions, but in many dimensions it becomes very complex.

The n dimensions of the space correspond to the features which are considered to make items similar. From observation of the positioning of products in this space, gaps will become obvious. Products can then be described which might fill these gaps.

Up till now, all that has been achieved in this model is the establishing of dimensions of products and the suggestion of products which have characteristics that are partially embodied in other products. In the next stage of the model, Stefflre tries to establish the consequences of introducing a product into this preference space.

From a 200-person national sample, rank orders of products and of the descriptions of features consumers in the smaller samples have mentioned as being embodied in the products are obtained. In Stefflre's model, products and descriptions of characteristics were then placeable in a three-dimensional space. Items and descriptions liked by the same individual are placed near each other. From this model, validation of previous results can be obtained (i.e. previous estimation of where a particular brand is located in the preference space of consumers and why it is so located). Also, potentially better information on the description of brands that might occupy gaps in the market structure becomes available, although the small number of dimensions (three) can limit the analysis.

The final step in the market structure study consists of testing a small number of new product descriptions, using the data from a large (1500) national probability sample to determine the proportion of people (to obtain the proportion of buying volume) that prefer each composite description to the brands that they currently use. If it can be assumed that buyers will actually buy a product of a preferred description if it is produced, then the products from which each theoretically described product will take sales and the increases and decreases in market shares of existing products can also be determined. When the method turns up a description which performs according to the aims of management, the next step is to proceed to an analysis of costs in order to estimate the feasibility of producing the product.

Stefflre's model is taken further by a procedure which helps the manufacturer to evolve the product, packaging and advertising, etc. that fits the new product description. To do this, various possibilities are presented to small samples of consumers, with possibilities embodying the descriptions in different ways. When this is done, a large-scale preference test is conducted to check that the product performs according to the description that it was designed to match.

An important characteristic of Stefflre's approach is that it introduces the idea of non-metric multi-dimensional scaling for us. Non-metric multi-dimensional scaling is a way of arriving at measures of similarity from a number of non-metrically (i.e. not measured in the usual scalar way) determined measures on different dimensions. One such technique starts with an arbitrary scattering of points with declared preferences between them and shifts these points until the pairs that were declared to be most alike are closest together in space and those least alike are farthest apart. The crucial point is that an *n*-dimensional spatial analogy is used for preferences (or whatever is used to rank products). Such a procedure is of obvious use in consumer theory.

We now have to consider what use Stefflre's approach is in extending the idea of abstract modes. The most obvious difference is that instead of operating on actual choices, it operates upon stated preferences. This is extremely useful for our purposes, since for most products the choice situation is less easily identifiable than with the transport choice, so it is better to present the consumer with an artificial choice and observe his decision and his account of it. One possible source of problems is that the breadth of the analysis is effectively determined by the consumer. For, throughout the analysis, the method concentrates on the consumers' own perceptions of product quality, rather than on the manufacturer's ideas for qualities to be embodied in products. It is only at the stage where the exact way in which qualities are to be combined is decided that creativity has a chance to enter into the analysis. Perhaps if characteristics of products were suggested to consumers (rather than asking consumers what characteristics products were considered to have), creativity would play a greater role. The inputs into the computations are not the absolute and relative characteristics of products as measured by an external analyst (as in the case of the abstract mode analysis), but consumers' perceptions of the characteristics of products relative to one another. It is clear that most firms would at the final stage want to test different product formulations as well as the one thrown up by the analysis, which would lead to much higher costs of analysis. The successive resampling involved in Stefflre's approach can be very expensive, but the saving of cost which could be achieved by cutting sample size would be very risky.

However, Stefflre's approach could be modified at most stages by the substitution of product characteristics that have been determined *a priori*. Although this would have the danger that the characteristics of products might be incorrectly chosen, it would considerably cut down the cost of the analysis. In addition, it would have the advantage that any product characteristics which manufacturers suspected of being too expensive to achieve could be eliminated at an early stage of the analysis, thus saving further costs.

In practice, however, techniques of the kind described above, although they will help the manager evolve ideas concerning demand for new products in a more rational way, may prove too expensive to all but the largest firms. For the manager with limited research resources at his disposal, the required data are too expensive to collect and it is unlikely that much of the required information, concerning (as much of it will) the details of preferences between different types of the same product, will be stored in data banks, although the day has been envisaged when a substantial amount of preference information will be stored and made publicly available. Even if such information is available, severe doubts exist about its stability. Normally, managers can rely on the stability of very general relationships, but very detailed preferences are unlikely to remain stable over time. By using categories of analysis which are evolved from studies of consumers, the advantage of using familiar categories is lost. A familiar category has the advantage that the way in which it is likely to change will be more or less well-known.

Given this qualification, the average manager will probably prefer to use a more subjective way of arriving at final demand figures at the most detailed level, sacrificing possible accuracy for ease and cheapness of analysis.

Instead of starting with preferences as expressed verbally, the manager must for reasons of economy start with current and past purchasing patterns. The firm already knows what the general trend in the market under investigation is, in particular the responsiveness of demand to income and the ways in which tastes are changing. Depending on whether the firm has already been involved in the area in question for some time, there may already be some information in its possession concerning consumers' reactions in the past to changes in competitive strategy. But, at a minimum, the firm will need to find out what the market shares of different types of product are and how they have changed in the past. It will also need to know how relative prices have changed and how much promotional effort the firms concerned have put into each product. This information will be very difficult to collect in markets where there is no continuing research by market research agencies. But unless the firm is to decide on its final choice of product specifications in the dark, the information is essential.

This gathering of information will have to be done for each of the narrow demand areas in which the firm is interested. Once this is done, the firm must then carry out a gap analysis, using its own terminology for the characteristics of products.

In each market, there will be products of several different prices, several levels of promotion and with some degree of product differentiation. The firm then has to investigate whether any large gaps appear in the analysis. For example, the firm might find out that there are high-price products and low-price products, but none in between. Or alternatively, it might discover that there were products of high levels and low levels of promotion, but few in between. It would then need to investigate why these gaps existed. The gaps will usually exist for some good reason, rather than because of some omission on the part of potential competitors, and these gaps will do a lot to explain which factors *in combination* are important in determining the sales of a product. This will help the firm to decide what sort of product price/quality/promotion combination should be tested. Small-scale tests can be extremely useful at this stage to establish the likely extent of demand, even in the case where samples of products cannot be produced, since product descriptions are often adequate for preliminary purposes. Statistical correlation of market shares with selling characteristics may be possible if some adequate variable can be found to represent product quality. But small-scale tests will be able to give a more reliable indicator of the *extent* of preference for any particular product formulation. If the firm is a completely new entrant into a product area, it may be safer to choose a specification which is likely to have a small but intensive demand, because of the risk of competitive intervention. At this stage, some idea of the restrictions that may be imposed by resources needs to be brought in, so the kind of considerations discussed previously will need to be raised again.

Normally, with this informal approach to the analysis of demand in a narrow market area, there will be more opportunity than in the formal models for the incorporation of qualitative information and for the process of adjustment between demand investigation and product formulation which must take place. Testing and retesting the product formulation finally decided for each market against demand is crucial here. It is also here that cost considerations must start to enter more formally. These we consider in Chapter 5.

DEMAND AND PRODUCT PLANNING: CONCLUSIONS
In this chapter, we have not tried to provide a formula for the firm to establish which markets it should be involved in and what kinds of products it should consider producing for them, subject to cost considerations being satisfactory. Rather, we have tried to outline the important considerations that must be taken into account if the firm is to orientate its product policy towards demand developments. There is no simple answer that can be given at this general level. Different methods will be suitable for firms in different situations. Techniques

of demand analysis are constantly being developed and described in the appropriate journals, but the important developments for the firm are likely to be in the area of data collection. As long as data sources are inadequate, the best that can be recommended is the subjective approach to establishing patterns of demand for new products, and the firm will always want to temper this with very strong resource limitations.

In this chapter, we first established the need to delimit the area for intensive demand research. This is done on the basis of broad research into the long-term prospects for different markets, as well as for the economy as a whole. If the aims of a firm are reasonably clear cut, in terms of what rate of growth it is looking for, then a short list of markets with the highest potential needs to be drawn up. The firm then has to investigate the extent to which it possesses a competitive advantage within each of these areas. This will depend on the difficulty that it and other possible competitors will face in moving from their current resource–product–customer base to the one required for the new market area. If a firm has a reasonable advantage in certain areas (and the criteria for this have to remain relatively indeterminate), then it needs to establish more clearly the future demand characteristics in these areas. In this chapter, we moved relatively rapidly from one stage to the next, but in practice firms will probably go through several stages, limiting the scope of research more and more at each stage. Firms should always be aware of the consequences of each delimitation and be ready to move back if they have reason to believe that a previous delimitation was too severe or not severe enough. This is particularly true where the firm is deciding in detail on demand areas to pursue, since choices will be highly sensitive to external developments. In addition, the data constraints will be so severe here as to limit greatly the reliability of any decision to restrict the area of research. These data constraints are also such as to make it very difficult to use any of the mathematical approaches to new product demand formulation. However, these approaches do at least suggest a logic of investigation to the practising manager, in particular the importance of relating rating of attitudes to rating of products. But the problem of stability of findings over time is a serious one too, such that more informal approaches may be more suitable because they make it easier for managers to estimate the consequences of changes in parameters. The way in which product demand changes over time is a subject of intense investigation by management researchers. This is considered in further detail in the next chapter.

4 The Product Life Cycle

The product life cycle is a notion which is frequently discussed in the literature of marketing management. According to the theory of the cycle, products are said to be on a market for a limited time, during which they pass through the phases of introduction, growth, maturity, saturation and decline. Booz, Allen and Hamilton[1] depict these phases as in Fig. 4.1. Their view of the sales and profit performance of products is shared by many writers.[2] If their view is correct, then the concept of the product life cycle must be of interest for managers in the process of setting up their product plan. If it is true that every market has a limited life, then this tells the manager something about the opportunities that are likely to become open to him and how long they are likely to last. There are also associated hypotheses concerning the type of managerial talent that is likely to be most in need at the different stages of the cycle. If the life-cycle theory has some validity, then it will obviously be of some use to the product-planning manager.

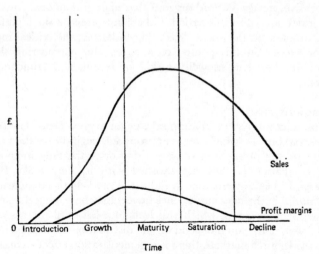

FIG. 4.1   The product life cycle

The first step in the evaluation of any theory of this kind, as far as its usefulness for management purposes is concerned, must be some test of its validity. We can summarise what we need to know about the cycle in two composite questions, as follows :

1. What theoretical reasons are there to expect products to follow particular sales and profit-margin patterns over time and, if particular patterns are to be excepted, what are the implications of these patterns?
2. What empirical justification is there for using the concept as a representation of a typical sales pattern and, if there is such a justification, how does it affect the description of the basic cycle?

Before attempting to answer these questions, we describe the basic features of the model.

The phases of the cycle are characterised as follows.

THE INTRODUCTION PHASE

In this phase, sales and profit margins are low. Sales are low because advertising and sales efforts, in both consumer and industrial markets, take time to create demand. Consumers and industrial buyers are reluctant to change to new and relatively unfamiliar products. Profits are low for several reasons. Initial expenditure on launching the product may be very high. For some consumer goods, media advertising may be extensively used, but the firm may also give large discounts to retailers in order to encourage them to stock up. There may be production difficulties in the initial stages and overcoming them may be an expensive process. Patton[3] suggests that high promotional costs make heavy losses normal in this period. Fisher[4] lays stress on the high failure rate of products at this stage. According to Patton, the critical ingredients for success in this phase are research and engineering skill in product development, as well as skill in testing and launching the product.

THE GROWTH PHASE

If the product survives its infancy, sales begin to grow faster. Consumers or industrial buyers (whichever is appropriate) begin to try the product (perhaps on the promptings of advertising or of the sales force of the selling company). If they are satisfied with it, they make further purchases. Fisher suggests that in industrial markets this may lead to a slight 'hump' in the sales curve, since buyers may be buying the product for assessment purposes, which will lead to a lag until the assessment is completed. This would depend on the distribution of such assessment purchases. In some markets, there is a demonstration effect – consumers see others buying the product and want to try it for themselves. For some products, further uses are found as users become more familiar with the properties of the product. Retailers and distributors at higher levels may initially have hesitated to stock the product, but as they see it make headway in the market, they may order larger stocks and give the product prominence in their displays. Profit margins of the manufacturing firm rise rapidly as promotional costs are spread over a quickly rising output (as are any fixed costs). There is also a learning effect on the production line (and perhaps in other areas) and this effect exerts a downward pressure on costs.

The price of the product is obviously a crucial determinant of the profit margin. It is apparently assumed that in the first two phases of the product cycle, the firm has relative freedom in setting the price. In the first phase it sets it low enough to encourage the growth of the market, but not so low as to incur large losses. In the growth phase, the price is high relative to cost in order to cover the cost of the investment, the cost of previous failures and to make profits before competition starts to erode the firm's advantage. Note that this does not mean that the price is absolutely increased, since costs may be dropping relative to it to achieve the higher margin.

In this phase, Patton says, the problem of management is to get a workable version of the product on to the market in a large enough volume to secure a brand franchise (this applies in particular to consumer products) and to build acceptance at the distributor, retail and consumer levels. The key function is therefore the manufacturing function. Patton states that many products have died because engineering or research personnel tinkered with the product design for so long that competitors pre-empted the market by the time production got under way.

THE MATURITY PHASE

Here competition begins to make itself felt. Other firms, having noticed the success of the product, enter the market with almost identical products (they may have already started to do this in the growth phase). By this time the growth rate of the whole market has begun to fall, as the unexploited potential which gave the market its high rate of growth early on begins to diminish. The rate of growth of the original firm's sales may fall quite sharply. It can no longer cream the market and must now devote more energy to promoting sales and retaining its position in distributive outlets. Before, all it had to do was to make sure that the product actually reached the outlets. In industrial markets (and to some extent in consumer markets) the quality of competing products becomes an especially important determinant of market share.

Though the original firm's sales may still be rising quite fast in absolute terms and in relation to the rate of growth of the economy as a whole, its profit margins begin to fall. It now has to increase its promotional expenditure or cut its price. The key function in this phase is, according to Patton, the marketing function, since by this stage most competitive products will be reliable and there will be relatively little to choose between them. Improvements in the product tend to be small, with selling features or styling changes predominant. As soon as the profit margin begins to fall, the firm should initiate plans for further product development.

THE SATURATION PHASE

In this stage, the demand for the initial firm's product will reach its peak. If there is no better product forthcoming, says Fisher, the total market for the product may rest on a plateau for some time. But, Randle says, as other firms are producing large quantities of the product, supply tends to outstrip demand, so that the initial firm's sales of the product begin to fall. Competition becomes intense in price, quality and promotion. By this time, newer products may be appearing, making buyers even more critical of the product's performance. Management should by this time be considering how to regenerate the product, for sometimes renewed expansion can be achieved by giving fresh thought to the product. Levitt[5] suggests that the firm should plan for this in advance.

THE DECLINE PHASE

At this stage, sales begin to fall faster. Newer products may not satisfy all the needs met by the original product, which may remain relatively strong in some market segments. The share of the market retained by the original firm's products depends on the firm's ability to keep costs down, which is therefore the critical ability at this stage. Patton says that there is no point in making minor changes in the product at great expense. He argues that there is a great danger that the orientation necessary for success earlier on in the product's history (research, engineering, manufacturing and marketing) will outlive its time. Management must make sure that it gets a good return on all its expenditure, by stringent cost accounting.

This completes the summary of the main features of the product life cycle as traditionally portrayed. Product-cycle theorists are aware of some of the problems inherent in the concept. If it is to be used by management in making product-planning decisions, there are at least two important questions that must be answered unambiguously. These are :

1. Which products are subject to the cycle?
2. How can management determine which phase any given product is in?

Despite the assertions quoted at the beginning of this chapter, to the effect that all products are subject to the cycle, some space is in fact devoted to explaining which products are subject to the cycle. Fisher admits that the products of some industries may not be subject to the cycle. Patton lists a number of characteristics which 'help negate the facts of the life cycle'. These include patents, a limited number of producers who are willing to live and let live, heavy brand-advertising expenditures and a dominant market share by a single producer. Some products are said to be less subject to price cutting at maturity, including products which are bought emotionally, frequently from habit or because consumers have a preference for the product which they cannot explain, as opposed to their making a more or less judicious comparison of the merits of competing products. There are also, of course, products whose sales fluctuate principally according to the state of the economy.

However, as Polli points out[6], there are important theoretical reasons why we might expect product life cycles to exist. The most important of these relates to the process of diffusion, which, whether it applies to biological, social or economic phenomena, often produces a time-distribution curve very similar to that produced in product-cycle theory. However, as we shall see later when we consider Polli's criticisms of the theory in detail, we need a very precise classification of products in order to be able to make some kind of generalisation about which products are subject to this process of diffusion and to the life cycle. Such generalisations, as Polli shows, are better based on extensive empirical analysis.

Levitt gives some definite criteria for determining which phase of the cycle the product is currently in. The location of the beginning of the growth stage is taken to be fairly self-evident. Sales begin to rise faster (though Levitt admits that this can be the result of the filling of the pipelines of distribution), it becomes easier to open new distribution channels and retail outlets and competitors begin to enter the market. The location of the maturity phase is also taken to be quite easy. Levitt says that the first sign of this is that most companies or households that were considered to be sales prospects will by this stage already be owning or using the product. Levitt does not mention the fact that the definition of 'sales prospect' depends entirely on the marketing strategy of the firm selling the product. The firm may decide, quite incorrectly, that the product has little chance of success in a particular segment of the market. Later, when pressure from other producers in the market becomes very strong, they may re-examine this market and find that it does have good prospects.

The signs that the product has passed through the maturity stage are excess capacity in some firms, concentration of production, price cutting and so forth. All these could easily happen at an earlier stage. In particular, concentration of production might arise simply because one of the firms involved in the market has sufficiently large financial resources to purchase some of its major competitors.

These problems may diminish for specific empirical analyses, but there are obviously some major difficulties in applying the concept to specific products, since so many of the signs which are supposed to indicate a particular stage of the cycle can be caused by other economic factors. The fact that these difficulties exist does not however make the concept useless. The fact that, for example, the trade cycle is said by some economists to be inherent in capitalist economies but is modified so much by the economic policies of governments in some economies as to make them totally acyclical does not mean that the concept of the trade cycle is vacuous when applied to these economies. To carry the analogy between the two types of cycle further, suppose that it could be shown that the sales and profit-margin curves for a particular product could be intelligibly discussed while abstracting from the marketing and production policies of the firm manufacturing and selling the product. In this case, the product life cycle could be given some meaning as an underlying force which firms do their best to modify in the appropriate places.

What the above implies is that some clarification of the status of the concept is necessary before we can proceed any further. For this, we need to investigate in detail some of the terms used, in particular the following : *product, new, sales* and *profit margin*.

PRODUCT

It is clear that the extent to which a product is subject to processes of diffusion and competitive action will depend on how broadly it is defined. If the product is a generic one (such as cars), then there will be fewer substitutable products than if the product is an individual brand. The exact effect of this will be considered when we consider the results of the empirical analyses that have been carried out. But clearly, *a priori*, we would expect an individual brand to have a more marked cycle than the generic product if there were any cycle at all.

NEWNESS

It is clear that a very precise definition of newness is necessary in order to determine which set of sales and profit-margin data the product life cycle is intended to describe, or at least underlie. The possibility of regenerating products has already been mentioned and it is clear, from the writings of product-cycle theorists, that there is an important distinction between the new and the rejuvenated product. The latter will have been introduced into a market which is already highly competitive and will start with an initially high sales level, an established distribution system and so on. Yet many products which could be called new also have these characteristics (for example, brands of grocery food introduced with a very high level of promotional expenditure).

Patton's definition of newness is that a new product is one which opens up an entirely new market, replaces an existing product or significantly broadens the market for an existing product. This definition clearly allows many rejuvenated products to qualify on the grounds that they replace an existing product. The other two criteria depend completely on the marketing strategy of the firm. In some circumstances, they may amount to nothing more than that a new product is a product that the firm which markets it decides to treat as new. The status of at least the first stage of the product cycle would be that it was completely determined by management policy.

Fisher recognises that the definition of newness raises problems. He admits that it is partly a question of management policy:[7] 'Many companies would not regard minor variations as creating a new product and would delegate authority for them to a Product Manager or other appropriate middle executive'.

Fisher's analysis of newness is based on a division of the concept of product into five elements, as follows.[8]

Basic core
This is defined as the main need that the product satisfies and the service it supplies to customers.
Primary differentiation
This is defined as the different ways in which various products satisfy the same core need. For example, if the basic core of our product were alcoholic drinks, the primary differentiation might be beer, wine, whisky, etc.
Secondary differentiation
This is what separates one model from another. In our example, these may be the major types of beer, wine, etc.

C

Tertiary differentiation

These are described as matters which do not affect the applications to which the product is suited, perhaps making it easier to use or improving its appearance. In our example, this might be the different brands of the good.

Service

This can add value to the product with no change in the basic physical composition. In our example, this might be the way in which the product is packed or the size units in which it is sold.

Fisher suggests that products with a basic core differing from those of established products in the company are new, as are most of those with primary differentiation. But note that he has related this to the present product line of the company. This may be all right for some usages, but for our purposes it is clear that what happens to a product when it is introduced into a market depends on how new it is relative to the market and not on how new it is relative to the firm that is introducing it. However, his classification might be of some use if we define the terms relative to the market or segment of market. This still leaves us with the problem of deciding whether a product which is new relative to the market as far as secondary and tertiary differentiation is concerned is to be considered as new. A slight alteration to a product which makes it easier to use may turn it into a completely different product from the point of view of some buyers and thus to a sudden increase in the demand for it. However, Fisher's definition at least has more content than that of Patton. It establishes that newness can be independent of technical change. But it still leaves us with a major problem in distinguishing which products are new. This is not just a semantic difficulty, for there are many situations where it is difficult to distinguish a new product from variations in existing products, even with the advantage of hindsight. This produces the possibility that there will be substantial error in assessing the future of an existing product. Promotional policy can obviously alter the extent to which a product is considered new by the market, therefore unless we have some way of taking this into account, the usefulness of the product life cycle is considerably diminished. As we shall see when we come to the empirical analysis, the problems in explaining behaviour are less severe when more rigorous statistical definitions are adopted, but they still remain.

SALES

The cycle is defined in terms of sales and profit margins, but it is not always clear at what level of distribution the sales are being made. The arguments for the shape of the curve being as depicted in Fig. 4.1 are mostly in terms of what is happening in the final market (consumer or industrial). There may be long lags in the distribution system, particularly if the product is traded on an international scale. If these lags are long relative to the 'life' of the product, manufacturers' sales may diverge considerably from the cycle pattern if the latter does exist at the level of the final market. Theorists of the cycle claim that there are both production and marketing consequences of the cycle, but they do not point out that particular distribution system can change the sequence. This is particularly important where the manufacturer has no quick way of discovering what is happening in the final market for his product, which is likely to be the case where there is more than one level of distribution between the manufacturer and the final customer. There are many ways in which the existence of other holders of stock (apart from the manufacturer) can affect the relation between manufacturers' despatches and final sales and these will depend upon factors such as the type of product (its unit value, frequency of purchase, etc.), the way in which it is promoted by the manufacturer and distri-

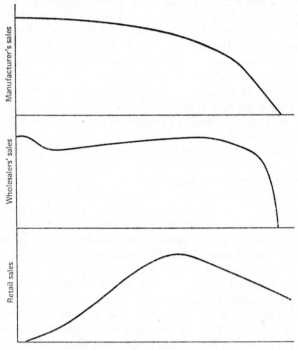

Fig. 4.2   Sales at different levels (i)

butors, the structure of competition in all the levels of the distribution chain through which it passes, the cost of handling stock (the bulk of the product, cost of space and of capital) and so on. There is not the space to discuss all these in detail. Instead, a hypothetical example will be used.

Suppose that a manufacturer who distributes his goods through wholesalers and retailers launches a new non-durable product. He gives the trade a preview of the product and asks them to put in an initial order, having assured them that the product will be well publicised. Suppose that retailers order high stocks from their wholesalers because they are convinced that the product will be successful. After the launch, retail sales start quite low. Though they soon begin to pick up, retailers do not need to renew their orders for some time. Wholesalers' sales show a sharp drop, but this is expected after the launch of any product. Because they expect a large number of repeat orders, they maintain their order levels with the manufacturer. But as the effect of the launch promotion begins to wear off, final sales do not increase very rapidly. The heavy initial level of promotion has been reduced and retailers are not drawing the attention of their customers to the product with as much energy as before. Wholesalers begin to get worried and cut their orders sharply. All this might give sales at the three levels as shown in Fig. 4.2. But the manufacturer's sales are also consistent with sales at the other two levels as in Fig. 4.3, where the product had a high level of sales initially. This level began to drop and retailers tried to maintain it by their own price cutting and promotion, which led to a slightly higher level, but then the decline reasserted itself and wholesalers in return were forced to cut their orders as retailers cut theirs.

It is vital that the manufacturer knows what is happening at the final sales stage. His sales are consistent in this case with either a life-cycle shaped curve or another shape. One interpretation of the difference between the two product histories might be that in the first the product was good but the promotional effort flagged too early, while in the other, though in the end a large number of people tried the product, it was not good enough to produce repeat orders on a sufficiently large scale. In the latter case, the crucial management skill required might be research and engineering, as well as production, so that the firm could quickly get an improved version of the concept, which did in fact have broad consumer appeal, on to the market.

Since, as this example shows, the type of distribution system can have an important effect on the relationship between final sales and manufacturers' despatches, even if the cycle does exist at final sales level, the output of the firm may be considerably different from that

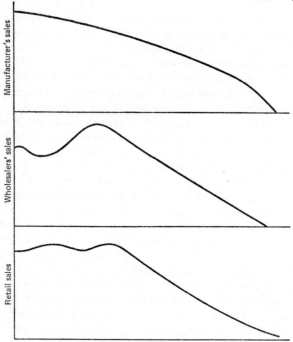

FIG. 4.3   Sales at different levels (II)

experienced by distributors. This has two consequences for product policy. First, analysis of the state of possible competitive products has to take into account differences of this kind. Secondly, the management of new products, which according to the theory has different requirements at different stages in the cycle, must be considered that much more carefully, since a high volume in the final market might not coincide with a high volume of output. In this case, different skills would be required in management.

PROFIT MARGINS

Profit margins play an important part in product-cycle theory, for it is their rise and fall which is supposed to determine the optimum policy of the firm. In particular, when the margin turns down, a new product should be ready for launching in order to maintain the profitability of the whole firm. As the margin gets lower and lower, this is a sign to the firm that it is no longer worth while expending a lot of energy on the marketing of the product and on producing 'marketable' variations of the product. Rather, the firm should cut all unneccessary expenditure and proceed to 'milk' the product.

The problem here is that the definition of profits is not made explicit. There are many expenditures on the individual product which come in large 'lumps' and which firms allocate to the product over relatively short periods, often on an arbitrary basis. The result of this is that the profit margin may appear to be weak when the underlying position of the product is still very strong, and vice versa. If management were to take the cycle at its face value and began to devote their energies to the 'next' product when the profit margin fell because of an allocation of this kind, they might prematurely abandon a product with good prospects. Of course, most managers are much more aware of the consequences of the allocation of large expenditures than this. So, in order to 'save' the concept of the product cycle for use here, it is necessary to introduce the concept of the 'underlying profit margin', which is determined by the allocation of expenditures on more rational grounds. For example, advertising expenditure is strictly an investment, since it usually produces an increase in the tendency of consumers to buy the product which lasts for longer than the actual campaign. Advertising expenditure should therefore be allocated over a longer period of time, according to its true depreciation (reduction in effectiveness). Although this may be difficult to calculate in practice, some rough calculations can be made. Investment in capital equipment is of the same nature, but here the calculations are easier to make. General overhead expenditures are also sometimes of the same nature. For example, much of the management time that goes into considering the problems associated with a product occurs at the beginning of its life. On the other hand, the investment of management time remains effective for much longer. In the case of products which have a long incubation period, this investment can be an important part of the initial cost. Sometimes, it may be justifiable to modify the concept of underlying profit margin by excluding certain overheads if they are much the same for all the products in the firm or market and instead using 'underlying contribution to overhead'.

There is undoubtedly a large range of products where the definition of profit margin raises no difficulty for the concept of the product life cycle, especially those where overheads are small and where capital and advertising costs are spread evenly over time (though this does not remove the difficulties associated with the distribution of the effects of such expenditures over time, since the result of this may be large changes in the profit margin in some periods). For some products, however, it is necessary to exercise considerable care in arguing from the state of profit margins to optimum policies. If the firm in the final stages of demand analysis were able to obtain some indication of the likely state of profit margins for prospective competitors products, it would have to take account of the points mentioned above before it drew conclusions about its own optimum policies from the state of these margins.

These, then, are some of the problems that arise when the terms used in the theory of the product cycle are examined. It is clear from this discussion that the interpretation and use of the concept is a more complex matter than the simple exposition of the cycle would at first suggest. The status of the concept as a whole must now be considered.

There are several possible views on the status of the product cycle. Its status can probably best be clarified by examining the following three views :

1. The product cycle represents what happens to every product. Though the length of the cycle varies, as does the relative importance of the different phases, the basic characteristics are still visible in the sales and profit-margin data for all products.

2. The product cycle describes what happens to many products that are marketed in a capitalist market economy. When it does not happen, there are always good reasons to explain the departure from the pattern.

3. The cycle is a drastic oversimplification. The progress of the sales and profit margins of a firm's product is just as much a consequence of the firm's own actions as of the market forces operating on the product. The cycle says nothing new.

The view taken by most theorists of the product cycle seems to oscillate between 1 and 2. It does not lie between them, for sometimes they write as if the cycle were one of the facts of life, while at other times they list the exceptions. View 1 can probably be dismissed out of hand. Even if the theorists themselves did not list the exceptions, it is easy to call to mind products whose sales and profit margins have fluctuated (for various reasons, including extensive promotional campaigns, changing cost levels, production difficulties, etc.) so as to make it very difficult to apply the concept of the cycle to them. An investigation of the definition of the terms employed by the concept suggests that it may be difficult to define the set of data to which the concept is meant to apply. The problem is made even more complicated when we take into account that even if the cycle were of this well-established status, a firm selling in several markets might not be aware of the cyclical nature of its product's performance because of the way the cycles in different markets overlapped. More importantly, it may base its policy on the theory's recommendations according to what is happening in one market when the indications from other markets are that another policy would be more appropriate, just as one firm in the U.K. nearly did when recommended by its consultants to phase out their major product because it was entering the saturation phase of the cycle when in reality in lower income markets the product was just going through the take-off stage. Since in general the managerial recommendations are very highly dependent on the unambiguous assignment of particular sets of data to particular phases of cycle, these recommendations must be rather suspect.

The middle view has rather more to justify it than the first. It is certainly true that there are some products which do have sales curves similar to that depicted in Fig. 4.1. Whether they have profit-margin curves as depicted depends entirely on the definition of the margin. In order to examine this second view of the cycle more fully, a better account of it needs to be given.

Suppose that a firm has just launched a new product. What will happen to the product will depend on whether such a product is already sold on the market and on whether it is replacing a product catering for the same need. If it is either of these, sales may start at an initially high level. Otherwise, they may start at a low level and grow quite fast if the product is a success. Sooner or later competitors enter the market unless the firm is able to protect its position in some way (for example, by using patents, threats or supply restrictions for vital inputs). The firm will then have to change its strategy and concentrate on maintaining its position in existing outlets instead of trying to secure new ones. This will involve a reduction in profits per unit sold (depending on the definition of profits). What happens to the firm's sales then depends upon what is happening to the overall market for the product. If the market is still growing, then so may the firm's sales of the product. However, at some stage the market for the product is bound to become saturated, so that the firm's sales levels will even out or possibly fall. There exists the possibility of regenerating the product, by changing it slightly to give it a new marketing appeal, or of finding a new market for it, in which case the firm's profits from the product may increase again. Finally, the firm's position will be eroded by further new products (unless it develops substitutes itself) and the product's sales will decay until it is finally withdrawn. Though it may be possible to pick out a most important managerial function for each stage of the cycle, this should be done with great care, for all sorts of factors can change the situation. A sudden increase in the cost of one of the inputs may make it imperative that a new manufacturing process be developed in a short time. As far as further new product development is concerned, though firms should be aware of the vulnerability of their products, they should not be too prepared to abandon products without investigating alternative markets and uses.

There is not the space to add the many more qualifications that this moderate view requires. However many qualifications are made, there are still some difficulties inherent in it. If managers are to use it as a guide to policy, they must be aware of all the factors that might lead to sales and profit-margin figures departing from the pattern. To specify all of these would reduce the cyclical nature of the concept to nothing, for the fact remains that there are very many products that do not in fact have cyclical sales patterns as described. Some managers are sufficiently aware of the factors affecting their sales and profit margins to do without the concept. Possibly others may find it a more sophisticated way of remembering that 'what goes up must come down' in their industry.

The third view also has something to be said for it. Basically, it asks for the so-called cycle to be set in the context of all the policy options that are open to the firm, given a wide range of assumptions about the way in which the firm is organised, what the motivation of its managers is, what its position *vis-à-vis* the market is and also for some clarification of why other firms in the market behave as they do.

Space prevents giving the complete account that this view requires, though some indication of its implications can be given. For example, in the growth phase of the cycle, the rate of growth of sales depends on how the product is marketed. It is true that in many consumer goods industries (e.g. grocery foods) new products tend to be launched with such a large sales effort that sales do indeed grow very rapidly. But some firms do not promote their new products in this way. Instead, relying on a well-established distribution system, they introduce the product with far less publicity, such that sales start at a level which is much the same for the rest of their products and continue that way until for some reason the product is withdrawn. The average profit margin for the product is not necessarily any lower than it would be if the company launched it with very heavy initial promotion, for although the period of very high profit margins is forgone, the period of moderate margins lasts much longer. Competitors are less attracted by moderate margins than by the high margins of fast-growth products. This does not mean, however, that a company which usually launches its products with heavy promotional expenditure can with impunity suddenly decide one day to launch its next new product with the minimum of publicity, for the distribution system may have adapted itself to deal only with products of high turnover but short life. There may also be good reasons for their refusing to stock low-turnover items (though whether low turnover of each item would be the result if all firms decided to reduce their initial promotional expenditure is another question, which would also have to be investigated). In other words, this view of the cycle would maintain that while for some products firms in practice have very little choice concerning their marketing strategy, the reasons for this should be thoroughly investigated and the status of the supposed cycle made clear.

This third view is more concerned with the status of the cycle as a socio-economic phenomenon, but it also stresses that better understanding of the phenomenon would help to clarify the way in which it could be used as a management tool. This view is certainly correct in stressing that there are many ways in which the history of the product can differ from the cycle. Ample demonstration of this point comes from the various empirical tests that have been carried out for a wide range of products. Perhaps the most important of these is the work of Polli,[9] of which we consider the basic outlines here.

In order to test the validity of the cycle, Polli adopts a fairly strict classification of levels of generality of products and a strict definition of the stages of the cycle. He distinguishes[10] between product *classes* (defined by the general need or function fulfilled by a product), product *forms* (defined by their main technological or physical characterisation) and *brands* (ultimate specification by means of trademarks), on the grounds mentioned earlier, that these different levels of product have different substitution characteristics and that therefore their sales behaviour over time is likely to differ. Polli recognises that there are problems in unambiguously assigning products to each category and that there is some need for personal judgement.

The stages of the cycle, if the investigation is to be comprehensive, have to be defined such that the definition can be unambiguously applied across a wide range of industries. Polli uses a relative definition, suited to application in a growing economy. The percentage change in real sales over each year of the test for all products of a certain class of goods sold in a well-defined market is measured. Rates of growth which were more than half a standard deviation below average were considered to show decline. Rates of growth which were more than half a standard deviation above average were considered to show significant growth. Rates of growth between these limits were considered to show maturity of the product. Polli also defines the sub-divisions of sustained, decaying and stable maturity for respectively small positive and negative and zero rates of growth relative to the average. The introduction phase was defined as the period when annual sales were less than 5% of the observed peak level. Polli recognises that these definitions may raise problems as far as the theoretical definition of the cycle is concerned, but these are not considered to be too serious.

The next and most crucial stage is to set out for each product the sequence of stages which it has been found to have passed through on the above definitions. This sequence is tested against a random sequence and the sequence that would be expected in the classic cycle (introduction, growth, sustained maturity, stable maturity, decaying maturity and decline, with any number of years to be spent in each stage) to check consistency.[11] The most important conclusions reached by Polli for our purposes are that the degree of consistency with the classic cycle varied with the level of the product (higher with forms than with classes) and with industry (higher with durables than non-durables). This has certain implications for management. For example, because product forms in some industries show consistency with the cycle, firms facing a decline in their brand should extend their product line by a brand in a new form rather than a brand in the same form.[12] But a more important contribution made by Polli's analysis, perhaps, is to show that if the definitions of the cycle's characteristics are drawn up carefully enough, then clear empirical conclusions about the cycle's validity in various conditions can be reached.

The management implications of Polli's findings in the area of strategic decisions depend crucially on management being able to forecast the likely relative performance of brands within forms and this in turn will depend on the quality of the information about the characteristic performance of products in the past. In particular, the firm would need to establish the difference between the performance of classes, forms and brand in the past. It would be essential to try and find out the reasons for certain patterns of behaviour (e.g. particular diffusion patterns or particular marketing policies) and whether these explanatory factors were likely to persist. It might for example turn out to be the case that there was no strong need to react to a competitor's product policy change because of the likelihood of a change in the nature of the most successful product form.

Polli's analysis does of course investigate the dependence of product cycles on strategy, as well as the existence of incomplete cycles. The concern here has been to give some idea of one writer's methodology for testing the concept. In more general terms, Polli's analysis gives a useful insight into the appropriate procedure for evolving, testing and using any concept based on archetypal sales patterns. For example, in durable goods industries, which were found to show very little evidence of the cycle, general patterns might be found by testing sequences of rates of growth for deviation from the random for different product levels. Although any patterns established in this way might be difficult for management to use, they would at least provide a useful addition to the understanding of the nature of markets and a reminder that the distribution over time of events can be a useful classificatory device.[13]

However, from the point of view of management seeking to predict the pattern of sales of their own products and that of whole markets and competitive products in order to establish the prospects for new products, the concept of the product life cycle is not of proven validity. Perhaps its major use is to serve as a heuristic device which reminds managers of the need to take certain factors into account when considering suitable market areas for a change in the direction of their product policy. Its major disadvantage is that, depending as it does for its validity for policy recommendations on the forecasting of profit margins and hence on the forecasting of costs, it gives little enough consideration to the cost side of the analysis. This is the function of the next chapter.

5 Costs, Constraints and Capacity

INTRODUCTION

One of the most important points that has arisen from the discussion so far is that, because of the costs of obtaining information and the uncertainty of the benefits of obtaining particular kinds of information, managers are forced to cut down their area of investigation. First, the firm has to restrict itself to growth areas in the economy, then to demand areas where competitive pressure is least or least important and finally to products which occupy exploitable gaps in the market or (which sometimes amounts to the same thing) to products which create new markets. But once the basic characteristics of the products which will go forward to the final stage of analysis have been decided in the course of the demand analysis, the firm is faced with two major problems. These are as follows :

1. *Total product specification needs to be decided*. The firm will know from its demand investigation what principal characteristics are required from each product, but it needs to decide in what form these are to be combined and what kind of leeway it has got in altering the product's characteristics if cost considerations so determine.

2. *The costs of production need to be estimated*. This involves decisions on capacity and production constraints, which in turn depend for their validity on demand estimates, which in turn depend upon prices and other aspects of the firm's policy, which will in turn depend upon costs, thus giving rise to a circularity into which the firm must break. Both these problem areas are interrelated. Product specifications have to be decided partly according to costs. If a particular product specification turns out to be too expensive when all the output calculations have been made, then there will need to be some alteration in it, which in turn will affect demand and hence the scale of output, which in turn will affect costs. Thus the circularity mentioned above exists

even at this stage. This circularity cannot be ignored. We investigate its nature in the section on costs and confine our remarks on the product specification problem to design and related questions.

PRODUCT SPECIFICATION[1]

First of all, it needs to be stressed here that we are concerned with products that have to be designed and produced before they are sold, although some of the following remarks may apply to custom-built products. In other words, we are principally concerned with products which are produced in large batches or by continuous mass production techniques. With these latter, there is obviously room for altering some characteristics of a pre-designed product to suit customer requirements (e.g. option packages for cars), but even here the range of possible alterations is limited.

The second point to note is that there is not necessarily a particular product characteristic that follows automatically from a particular demand characteristic, unless the demand characteristic is very closely defined. For example, if a firm contemplating a move into the instant dessert segment of the grocery food market discovers a hitherto un-satisfied demand for a particular flavour, texture and sweetness, there will normally be several ways in which the firm can meet that demand. This means that there is room for creativity and original thought. More than that, these are really essential elements in the process of product planning. By their very nature, however, they cannot be planned. The creative process does not just consist of turning out ideas, which can to some extent be planned, but also of giving some direction to these ideas.[2]

Even if this process cannot be planned, there are at least some ways of ensuring that creativity can exist within a firm. For example, it is widely held that a stable environment within the firm provides the best setting for creative work, for then the planning/design personnel can take their environment as given and proceed with their creative work. Another view is that the firm should always maintain some organisational excess capacity, so that the various characteristics of the creative process can be allowed for (e.g. irregular progress and extraordinary costs). This is to some extent associated with the first idea, since if the firm has no organisational excess capacity, the people who should be doing the creative work will often be involved in ensuring that the firm is able to cope with day-to-day eventualities. In other words, they are not able to take their environment as given.

A fundamental distinction has to be made between creativity which involves substantial technical innovation and creativity which does not. In some cases, creativity consists of using an idea which is already in use in another market, for another product, etc. In this case, the creative idea is one of creative application. Some creativity involves using an idea for the first time ever, or else arriving at an idea individually. In the first case, creative search is the principal component of the creative process. This entails having good ideas about which existing techniques might be appropriate for another use. In the second case, it is more a question of finding and using personnel who can by themselves conceive and develop ideas for solving problems and discover new techniques for implementing ideas. Some conception of the variables involved here can be gathered from the extensive literature on the subject.[3]

If it is supposed that the firm has decided, for each of the product areas in which it is intensely interested, that the product to be sold in that area would have to have certain specific characteristics, are there any general or specific design rules which will guide the creative process (remembering that such rules need to be applicable to product areas in which the firm has not been previously involved)?

In principle, satisfactory design rules cannot be laid down in advance. If such a set of rules existed, then most of the firm's commercial problems would be resolved. The most we can say here is that there are certain suggestions that should be considered by the firm. Perhaps the most important of these is that design objectives need to be very clearly specified in terms of the demand characteristics thrown up by the previous analysis. This does not mean that a firm is always obliged to follow the demand analysis slavishly. A firm is often quite capable of altering the extent to which consumers want certain characteristics, especially if it is either first into the market or already holds a strong position in the market in which it is introducing the product. The strength of the firm's promotional effort in this respect should not be underestimated. What this means is not that the firm should go ahead and design independently of demand analysis, as far as the details of the product are concerned, but instead that it should try to analyse the extent to which consumer preferences are alterable and the dimensions along which they are alterable.

The second important consideration here is that at the design stage the firm needs to bear its market objectives very strongly in mind. There is often a tendency to design products which are likely to be *acceptable* to the bulk of the consumers in a particular market rather than to design one which will be very much favoured by a smaller number of consumers, without investigating the commercial logic of this. High acceptability is usually associated with more freedom in pricing. Although there may be in the end sound reasons for going for the first type of product, the feasibility of the second needs to be borne in mind. Safety is not always to be sought in a high sales level. For it may be that, if the firm is one of the first to develop a new market which demand analysis has shown to exist, long-term objectives can better be served by the design of a high-appeal minority product, to be followed by a mass-appeal product, given the tendency of consumers to make associations between products from the same manufacturer. Clearly, such choices can only be resolved finally when the cost analysis is taken into account.

COSTS OF DIFFERENT SPECIFICATIONS

If we assume that the firm has arrived at a number of design specifications which appear to be suitable for the markets which it is investigating, the next stage is to cost the alternatives. As was mentioned briefly before, this is an extremely complicated issue, because of the way in which the different components of the analysis are related. Let us restate the problem.

The costs of producing a given design will depend partly on the scale of production of the product. This is because as the scale of production of the product increases, the cost of fixed capital, overheads attributable to management, promotion, design and the like, and possibly raw materials costs will fall per unit produced, either because they are simply shared over a larger number of units, or because of bargaining with suppliers (especially in the case of raw materials), or because there are increased efficiencies to be had from larger production runs. But the scale of production of the product (both in terms of the amount produced over its whole life, which determines some economies of scale, and in terms of the amount produced per time period, which determines other economies of scale) will in turn depend upon demand. Although it may be possible to concentrate production within a smaller production period and thus achieve a larger output within that period, selling off the accumulated stock as determined by demand, in the main production and demand will be strongly associated, especially in the long term. Demand in turn will depend upon (among other factors) price and promotional expenditure. These are both in turn dependent on costs. Promotional expenditure is obviously dependent on costs, partly because it is an element of them and partly because promotion is often decided on the basis of what other costs are incurred by the product. Price is dependent on costs in a more complicated way. Manufacturers must usually allow for an appropriate profit margin on top of costs, and this margin together with the costs determines the price. But, as mentioned at the beginning, costs are dependent on production. There is therefore a circularity in the process of cost determination.

In economics, such an interdependence is usually resolved by resorting to the idea of simultaneous relationships, which are solved by the use of simultaneous equations. For example, suppose that for a given product variation, the average costs of producing and selling it for a typical year could be depicted by the curve CC′ in Fig. 5.1, assuming that the firm had made an appropriate decision about the level of capital equipment to be used in its production. Suppose too that the demand for the product were given by the curve DD′, assuming a certain level of promotional expenditure, the cost of which had already been included in the cost curve. Given these two curves, how would the firm then go about deciding upon its level of production, which would simultaneously determine costs and prices? Or, put alternatively, how would the firm fix its price, thus simultaneously fixing sales and production? Assuming that sales were not affected by any competitive reaction to the level of price set, then the simple view would be that if the firm aimed to maximise its profit for the period in question, it would have to maximise the area of the rectangle bounded by the two curves (as shown in Fig. 5.1). This can be done by simple calculus.[4]

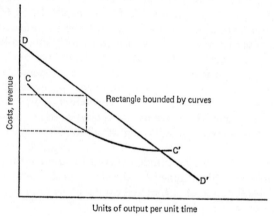

FIG. 5.1   Costs and demand

Notice that in the above analysis we assumed that the level of capital equipment was fixed and that the level of promotional expenditure was included in the cost, its effect on demand already having been taken into account. This we had to do because we depicted the situation in a two-dimensional diagram, and could therefore show only the impact of the variation of two variables. In fact, we can show the impact of changes in the promotional variables by introducing shifts in the curves, as depicted in Fig. 5.2. Here, the curves CC′ and DD′ show the level

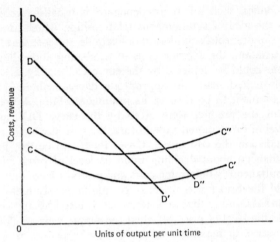

Fig. 5.2   Shifts caused by promotion

of cost and demand at one promotion level, while CC″ and DD″ show the result of a higher promotional level. We can still find out which is the maximum level of profits by comparing the maximum rectangles, but this involves us in an infinity of comparisons, especially when we start varying the level of plant, which we have assumed to be fixed. In fact, this problem is best represented by a set of simultaneous equations, which we solve for price, output, capacity, promotional expenditure and (if we could ever measure it) product design. But in order to set up this system of equations, we should need to know in detail the relationship between the following variables :

> *price and demand* (the simple demand function for the product);
> *price and cost* (determined by the firm's profit aims, presumably a complex function of output and capital expenditure);
> *promotion and demand*;
> *promotion and cost*;
> *capital expenditure and demand* (related through output);
> *capital expenditure and costs* (the cost of capital equipment and – when we take into account the time dimension – interest rate considerations);
> *product design and demand*;
> *product design and cost*.

As in the demand analysis, the major problem is information, but here the problem is much more serious, for as long as we lack information on one relationship, the others become difficult to establish. In theory, since we have six variables in the system that have to be established, we need at least six of the equations. Information of the appropriate quality is simply not available to firms. In addition, it should be remembered that we have assumed that we are discussing just one time period. When we take into account the point that we have to make the decisions for all the time periods in the product's life and realise that there is interdependence between the different time periods (the extent of success in one period will affect success in the next period, for example), then the system of equations becomes unviable, and we have to seek an alternative method of solving the whole complex of problems. The method we are forced to use is one which is not technically the best, but which involves a substantial amount of guesswork and successive adjustments over the life of the product. But it is held here to be the only practicable way for most firms to establish their cost levels in a non-arbitrary fashion. In analysing it here, we hope to bring out the possible sources of error and suggest how firms can correct for them. But first we consider the notion of opportunity costs.

The reason why we need to establish the costs of different product possibilities is that a decision has to be made about which possibility to take further. We are therefore seeking costs figures which are appropriate for making a decision. We are not, as so often when we are using cost figures, trying to present a report of the past activities of the firm. Therefore any cost figures that we use must represent what the firm is sacrificing by using a given resource. Just as we used the notion of the opportunity cost of capital when discussing the aims of the firm because it represents what the firm can do with profits over a particular period, so here we use the notion of opportunity costs of all resources.

Defined more exactly, the opportunity cost of a resource is the benefit the firm could have gained from using the resource in its next best use. Unfortunately, the cost figures available to firms are not usually based on opportunity costs. In the case of resources which are bought for immediate input into the production process, such as raw materials, there is no reason to expect this to differ significantly from the purchase price. This is because such inputs are bought with cash or other monetary resources, the opportunity cost of which is defined as the alternative use of the cash, which would be to buy resources of the same value. However, if there is some restriction on the amount of cash which the firm can obtain (through some form of capital rationing) then the opportunity cost of cash may be higher. This makes sense because it would tend to divert firms away from product possibilities which were cash-intensive to product possibilities which were not.

More problems are raised by resources that are already in use by the firm. These include capital equipment diverted from other uses and nearly all categories of overhead costs, in particular management costs. Here, the usual accounting cost figures will need to be modified by some consideration of the opportunity cost of the resources. For example, if management resources are diverted to the new product project, they should not be valued at the cost of salaries, but rather according to an estimate of what could otherwise have been done with them. This does not mean that if they were previously effectively unemployed within the firm they should be valued at a low level. There may have been other plans for using them. It is only if the resources have already been paid for or if the firm cannot escape payment for them (e.g. because of contractual obligations) *and* if the firm has no alternative use for them (for example, a piece of equipment with a highly specific use, bought for a project which was subsequently discontinued) that the value of the resources can be considered to be zero (which means that any employment of them will be beneficial).

However, this opportunity cost definition, which is in principle the best for decision-making purposes in the sense that it will lead to the most efficient use of resources (other things being equal), does give rise to some problems on the accounting side.

Suppose that a firm is considering the introduction of a new product and needs to set up a marketing team for it. The firm evaluates the performance of its marketing staff engaged on other products and finds that several managers can be transferred to this new product project without loss in performance of other products. If there is no alternative use for these managers (for example, if no other new product project is likely to be feasible and if no way can be devised for improving the managers' usefulness for existing products), then these managers can be considered to be a free resource, effectively paid for by the firm's existing products. If the new product project is adopted, then careful watch has to be kept on the performance of existing products to check that they remain able to carry the costs of the transferred managers. In other words, it is only worth embarking on the new product project (assuming that if the managers had to be fully paid for by it, it would not have been worth while) if the old products continue to pay for the transferred managers, assuming the firm's aims to be profit-orientated. So although the opportunity cost method of analysis is more efficient, it imposes a greater burden on the information system of the firm.

Having considered the basis of the analysis, we now turn to a consideration of the individual elements of costs. These are as follows :

Capital equipment costs;
Raw material and direct labour costs;
Management, marketing and promotion costs;
Distribution costs;
Finance costs.

This characterisation is not exhaustive, but it covers the most important categories of cost. We consider each of them in turn.

CAPITAL EQUIPMENT COSTS

Capital equipment costs will depend crucially on the level of capacity decided upon by the firm for each product possibility. This in turn, as we pointed out before, will depend upon the anticipated sales level for the product, which depends upon all the other factors in the analysis. Somehow, given the impossibility of solving this interdependence simultaneously, the decision has to be taken.

There can be no general principle to guide the firm for this estimate, which has essentially to be somewhat arbitrary. The main objective of the firm is to get some estimate of the likely range of sales values which is going to enable it to achieve its aims. Now, if there is no easily identifiable market for the kind of product possibility being considered, this will be very difficult, as there will be no indication from products currently on the market concerning the kinds of sales levels which can be achieved by products with particular design, pricing and promotional characteristics. The only guide will be the demand analysis previously carried out. This will give some idea of the price possibilities at different levels of sales. The firm has then to do some preliminary investigation of capital equipment possibilities. Perhaps the best policy here is to choose several different levels of output, investigate the costs of providing capital equipment for each level and see if there is any major infeasibility attached to any particular level of equipment provision.

If there are already some products in the market area (and this will usually be the case) the firm needs to build up a comprehensive picture of feasibilities before proceeding with the capacity decision.

The firm should proceed to choose several different levels of production per time period. If there are well-established products already in the market area, these levels should be chosen within those spanned by the products presently on the market, generally within the range of products considered to be most successful. At each level of sales chosen (and the number of sales levels chosen will have to be restricted by the information-gathering resources of the firm), the firm should make an estimate of the various costs associated with production for that sales level. This means comparing different techniques of production that would be suitable for each level and calculating all the associated costs. The major problem here is the level of marketing and promotional expenditure. The firm will have to estimate what level of expenditure would lead to the sales level assumed. In some market areas, some guide may be obtainable from the performance of other products. Otherwise, the firm will have to estimate it from the promotional characteristics of similar products. Similar in this context refers particularly to the distributional characteristics of the product, since these are the most important determinants of promotional policy.

Once the firm has obtained information on the consequences of several possible capacity levels, it will obtain some idea of the range within which the capital equipment that it finally sets up will have to produce. Given the likely inaccuracy of the information, there is no point on insisting upon too fine a tuning of the decision. But the firm needs to bear in mind the possibilities of divergence from the budgeted level of sales and the consequences of this for costs, before making the final choice of capacity level. Suppose that the firm has established that the likely range of production in a typical period after the product has been launched will be QQ', as shown in Fig. 5.3. Suppose, furthermore, that it has investigated three possible ways of producing within this range, the designed capacity levels for these three ways being taken as the upper limit of the range, Q'.

Choosing the upper limit of the range as the designed capacity level is not essential, but it is a reasonable step to take. First of all, the

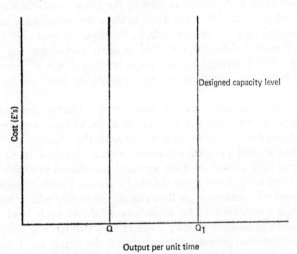

FIG. 5.3   Likely range of production

marketing costs of running short of supplies can be very heavy in the initial period of a product's life. Secondly, there are ways of running over capacity levels which may not be too expensive (for example, overtime working or producing in slack periods) in the short run, but which may be prohibitively expensive in the long run. Thirdly, capacity costs are often not a very sizable part of total costs, yet capacity can be extremely difficult to acquire, so that it is not worth risking undersupply for relatively little cost. Of course, certain types of capacity may be very expensive to obtain, while the firm may rate the probability of going over the maximum of the sales range as being very low, in which case the capacity chosen will be lower than Q'.

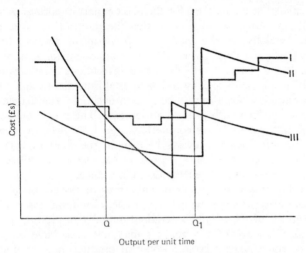

FIG. 5.4   Average capital costs per unit

Let us now suppose that these three ways of supplying capacity have average capital costs per unit per period of time as indicated in Fig. 5.4 by the curves I, II and III, which have different characteristics according to the ease of acquiring more capacity, the blocks in which capital comes and the original costs of the equipment, which may represent a more or less labour-intensive technique. The firm will then have to choose between techniques according to the other costs associated with production levels on and around the range QQ' and the estimated probability of being at certain points in or outside the range.

The important point to remember about any such analysis is that once the behaviour of capacity costs in a typical period has been established, the firm has also to establish their behaviour in the introductory period for the product, which may be a sizable part of its life. Costs incurred in the present are more significant than the same costs incurred in the future as far as the cash flow of the firm is concerned, and if these costs are net costs, because in the early stages of the product's life the firm will not be covering all its costs, then they are that much more significant. The firm should therefore pay considerable attention to the way in which these costs vary in the initial stages of the product's life.

RAW MATERIAL AND DIRECT LABOUR COSTS
These do not present so much of a problem as they are less likely to vary with the level of output of the firm's product, unless there are imperfections[5] in the markets for them. The most important point here, especially in an age of inflation, is that the result of any cost estimate depends crucially on the quality of forecasts of future cost levels. Labour, being the most important cost component for most products, can usually be forecast only by using projections of the rate of inflation of labour costs and by trying to establish whether the groups of workers employed are likely to be able to negotiate a settlement which is at all out of line with general settlements. The firm should not rely on wage settlements being counterbalanced by a general inflation of prices, for this does not always happen in the short or even in the medium term, and the life of a product may be virtually over within the period during which the balancing takes place.

The other important problem that arises in respect of labour and raw material costs is not the costing problem itself, but the establishing of how much of the inputs is required actually to produce a product which at this stage of the analysis may not even have reached the prototype stage, since a large number of products may be under consideration. This may not be too serious a problem for product projects which are in some way similar to products already being produced by the firm, but for others the only guide, apart from that available from the firm's own internal expertise, may be random pieces of information obtained from other industries. The crucial point here, given the likelihood of error in estimation, is to ensure that the error does not differ too much between product projects, especially between product projects which are more related to the firm's current activities and those which are less related. If the past records are available, the firm should try to establish what kind of errors it made in the past in estimating the costs for product projects which were similar to its existing products (taking into account the effect of inflation and other variables on the desired technique of production) and compare these with the errors it made on less familiar projects.

MANAGEMENT, MARKETING AND PROMOTION COSTS

There are several problems inherent in the establishment of these categories of costs. The common characteristic here is that all the categories leave the firm with a tremendous amount of leeway in making the estimate, both in deciding what physical level of the category is to be used and in deciding how much to spend on obtaining this level. In addition, these categories more than any other are likely to be shared with other products and therefore raise problems of cost allocation.

Take, for example, promotional costs. The firm has got to establish what level of promotion would have achieved an assumed sales level which is being used as the basis of other cost calculations. The firm must first try to establish, by inspecting the behaviour of similar products, roughly what kind of promotional level is going to be involved. In this context, similar must mean similar as far as type of product (durable or non-durable, frequency of purchase, type of use), type of market (frequency of purchase in particular, characteristics of buyers) and type of distributional system (kind of outlets, order structure, levels of distribution system) are concerned. The firm must try to infer from these (unless the product is very similar to one it is already producing) what kind of promotional levels would tend to produce the appropriate level of sales, given assumptions about consumers' willingness to buy. This analysis is bound to involve a substantial amount of guesswork, but if the data are available, the firm may be able to run some correlation analyses for changes in market share and promotional expenditure. However, this latter assumes the decision concerning what kinds of promotion should be bought. Promotion is not a variable that can be easily measured, so in principle the firm should also try to establish the effectiveness of the different methods of promotion separately.

Firms should not, as they often in practice do, try to dodge this issue by allowing a given percentage over other costs for promotional expenditure. Every effort should be made to establish what level of promotion would be *needed* to achieve the assumed level of sales.

The problem of *shared costs* arises for two reasons. Firstly, promotional effort is undertaken not just on a product basis but also across the whole product range of the firm. The promotion of some possible new products will normally be easier to integrate into the promotional programme of the firm than others, and will involve less cost. Here, the opportunity cost analysis is important. If the firm has a house name which is used successfully as a selling point, then that house name is a resource, commonly termed goodwill, and like any other resource it can be used up. But here the using up of the resource takes a slightly different meaning. For example, distributors might be unwilling to

stock more than a certain number of products of one brand name, be-
lieving it their duty to offer the customer a wide range of choice. This
applies especially if distributors are shops with limited shelf space.
Even where space is not limited, distributors might find it convenient
to ration the number of products taken up from one company. Less
frequently, if a product's performance falls below the expected level
for the consumer, then goodwill can be used up in a very real sense.
Somehow or other the opportunity cost of using up this goodwill must
be calculated, through expected loss of profit through loss of sales of
other products, according to some estimate of the probability of distributors deleting products or reducing promotion of the firm's other products and according to the risk of loss of sales of existing products
if the product fails.

Management costs, like promotion costs, present a particular problem
as far as their distribution over time is concerned. The amount of
management effort required in launching a product will differ considerably from the amount of effort required to maintain the product
in sale. The management effort in the initial stages will therefore
usually partly consist of managers diverted from regular work elsewhere or, given the fact that it is rather expensive to expand the management team temporarily, the managers will be part of a team set up
to help with the launch of new products. There is thus either an
opportunity cost problem or a problem of cost sharing (with other new
products).

The cost-sharing problem is always one that raises difficulties for
rational decision-making. If it is really impossible to allocate costs on
the basis of the true incurring of costs, then usually some arbitrary
method has to be resorted to. For example, suppose that new products
marketing is the responsibility of a particular group of marketing managers, who after the product is established hand over responsibility for
it to another team. How are the costs to be allocated between the
different products launched by the group? If there were records available of the amount of time and other resources used by the group on
each product possibility, then the allocation could be achieved on a
rational basis. But if not, then the firm should assume that each product
has made an equal call in absolute terms on the resources of the team,
unless there are good reasons for assuming otherwise. The firm should
therefore allocate an equal lump sum to the cost estimates for each
product possibility, rather than a proportional mark-up on sales revenue
or on other costs.

Development costs, which can be regarded as a particular aspect of
management costs, are always a difficult item to deal with. First of all,
their level is both in principle and in practice very difficult to estimate,

unless a firm is dealing with a type of product with which it is very familiar. The firm has to try and forecast to what extent it will run into problems, what sort of costs will be incurred in trying to solve these problems and so on. If a firm in the motor industry is considering launching a new car model, it can budget fairly realistically for development costs, since it knows what sort of problems are likely to arise. But a diversifying firm will have to rely on information obtained from other firms. It may find it worth while to hire managers from other firms simply to improve the quality of information input at this stage.

DISTRIBUTION COSTS

Unless the firm is effectively the distributor of its product direct to the final buyer, the distribution system for the product will involve an active third party as an intermediary. The distribution system chosen for a product actively transforms the nature of demand and does not just play a passive role. Thus any demand estimates have to be altered so that they are seen as the outcome of the buyer's pressure on distributors. Especially in industries where distribution is concentrated and where the choice of products available to the consumer may effectively be decided by a few people, this makes forecasting the reactions of distributors a crucial element in demand forecasting, an element which is frequently overlooked. This will involve a substantial amount of product concept testing with potential distributors, in order to see which distributors will be the most receptive to different product formulations. This in turn will determine the costs of distributing the product. The firm has to establish what sort of promotional discounts and other incentives will need to be offered to the distributors to achieve the assumed sales level. Of course, these costs will be to some extent substitutable for other costs. More promotion costs will mean that less will need to be spent on promotional discounts, since distributors will see higher promotional expenditure as a guarantee of a higher turnover and higher profits for them.

FINANCE COSTS

Finance costs are defined as the cost of financing any deficit between receipts and expenditures. They therefore do not just concern capital costs, but the total cash flow due to the product possibilities under investigation. The possibility of a deficit in any particular debt settlement period (the period within which borrowings do not have to be paid for) arises not just during the launch of the product but also when any major updating of capital equipment is necessary.

As we pointed out at the beginning of Chapter 2, finance costs are not simply related to the cost of borrowing or the yield from lending on the open market at any particular time. More often than not, capital rationing of some kind exists, whether this is imposed by the stock market or by government action.

This means that the firm has to take into account its own likely net cash surplus position in any debt period before evaluating the true opportunity cost of capital. This will depend on the size of the project relative to the firm's total activities, the likelihood of attempts by outside agents to obtain control and the importance of control as a business aim, as well as the standard variables of current market borrowing and lending rates. These latter in themselves may be difficult to establish, but the firm may be able to rely on government or other research reports for this purpose.

Having established the major characteristics of costs for each product possibility within the appropriate rate of production in each time period, the firm then needs to make a rough summing of these categories of costs. The firm must also carry out a sensitivity analysis of costs. This means that it must try to establish what limits there are to possible variations in the estimated costs, and then establish the total effect of these variations on the final estimated cost figure. For example, if labour costs were estimated to be 50% of the total costs for one production technique for one of the product possibilities, but the firm estimates that there is a possibility that wage inflation will take this to a higher proportion, then this figure should be included as a maximum cost estimate to be taken into consideration when the final decision is made.

The information required for an adequate cost analysis is very substantial, so at this stage the firm should consider whether there are any constraints it can impose on the analysis without excluding too many opportunities which might lead to greater satisfaction of aims.

CONSTRAINTS

There are several possible constraints that a firm might impose on itself via the cost analysis. These will include considering products that will yield a minimum of sales, carrying out promotional policies by certain methods only, using only certain kinds of production method. We cannot cover all the constraints that firms might impose. Here we consider the most important constraints that emerged in the empirical survey for the book.

SALES CONSTRAINTS

When considering the cost characteristics of a new product, the firm has, as we have seen, to make some assumption about the kind of sales level with which it will be dealing. Some firms actually impose as a constraint that the firm should not consider a product which is likely, under various assumptions about pricing, promotion and distribution policies, to produce less than a certain annual sale. This constraint enters the analysis at this stage (sometimes as early as the demand analysis stage) by the firm's refusing to investigate the cost characteristics at levels below this. If in subsequent stages of analysis the product does not prove to be viable within the sales range investigated, then the firm proceeds no further with the investigation, without having a look at the possibility that it could produce and market the product successfully at a lower volume.

Can this practice be justified in any way? Given that there are management economies of scale in dealing with fewer products and given that management may be the most crucial resource limitation on strategic possibilities, there may be some justification for a minimum sales constraint on the grounds of the limited capacity of managerial resources.

The problems of management resource limitations have already been discussed in this book, but here the firm should make a very determined effort to establish the relationship between managerial effort and returns. There is no necessary correlation between time spent on a product and success, nor is there any necessary correlation between sales and success, unless the success criteria of the firm explicitly include sales. The problem here is that many firms have got used to the idea of a relatively fixed relationship (at least in normal times) between sales and profits, such that a policy which produces the most sales per unit of management input is also assumed to produce the largest profit per unit input. This is by no means necessarily the case. Especially if the firm is considering moving into a new market area, it needs to consider the relationship between profit and sales in both the long and the short run, and then to consider the impact of managerial input on both.

Sales limitations may have more justifiable bases. For example, distributional factors of the kind already mentioned in this chapter may make a minimum sale per product an inevitable requirement (e.g. if distributors ration exposure and stocking). But this policy may sometimes be a misguided one on their part, due to *their* assuming the existence of a stronger relation between profits and sales than actually exists. If the role of the premium product (especially in developing a new market) is properly recognised, then such limitations may be better avoided.

Sometimes sales restrictions on the product possibilities considered may be based on intimate knowledge of the cost conditions prevailing for the product. These may show that a product of below a certain volume is unlikely to be saleable profitably because of the very high unit costs that prevail at low volumes (perhaps because of the nature of the capital equipment needed to produce the product). A good example of this would be the motor industry and the introduction of a new car model. At the same time, familiarity with only one type of production technology (say, one based on mass production) may lead a firm to ignore the possibilities of alternative technologies.

PROMOTIONAL CONSTRAINTS

In many industries it is accepted that there are certain ways in which products should be promoted. These ways are built into cost estimates. Take for example the tradition of exposure of new models at motor shows in the car industry. It has been less favoured recently as firms have faced financial problems, but it is interesting to note how long this tradition persisted before it was questioned. It was by no means proved that this was the best way of spending the promotional budget, nor were the amounts spent (which were very sizable) subjected to much analysis. It is true that many firms feared that if they themselves ceased to exhibit, their competitors would gain sales, but it was not proved that other means of promotion could not make up for this lack of exposure. There is tremendous inertia in decision over promotion, perhaps because a firm's promotional decisions are subject to pressure from outside agencies, in whose interest it is for the firm to persist in their current pattern of expenditure.

PRODUCTION METHOD CONSTRAINTS

These have already been mentioned in the context of sales constraints. They can occur at any level, from the distinction between mass production and small batch production to distinctions between the use of different types of labour and management methods. These enter into cost estimates through the firm's assumption about the appropriate methods and the costs attributable to them. Much the same points arise here as in connection with promotional methods. The firm should seek to establish the basis of any assumption it makes before proceeding on that assumption. Certain cases of dramatic changes in production technology have received great publicity (for example, the use of group technology[6] in the place of mass production techniques), and these cases bring out the point that one of the best times to make a change in production technology, payment systems, promotional methods and so forth is when a new product is being introduced. Unfortunately, the riskiness of the whole business of introducing a new product tends to push the firm towards playing safe in as many ways as possible. But it is fair to suggest that the firm should consider taking advantage of the flexible environment that the introduction of a major new product will produce to make any changes of this kind that have already been found to be worth while.

COSTS, CONSTRAINTS AND CAPACITY : CONCLUSIONS

In this chapter we have tried to indicate some of the major points that need to be taken into account when the firm is making its cost estimates for the several new product possibilities that it is assumed to have under consideration. First, it was pointed out that there is no essential link between demand characteristics and product specifications. Creativity has a crucial role to play in the process, and the very essence of creativity is that it cannot be planned. But once the specification(s) have been fixed, however temporarily, the firm faces an almost insoluble problem of interdependence between all the policy variables which it has under its control. This interdependence can only be broken into (given the lack of adequate knowledge about the relationships involved) by making certain crucial assumptions about sales, production and promotion techniques (among other factors) and investigating the viability of the product possibilities on the basis of the cost figures derived after making these assumptions. Perhaps the most crucial point of all is that the assumptions that have been made need to be borne constantly in mind. Managers need to restate each time any decision is made what the basis of the decision is, and then try to see what the sensitivity of the decision is to relaxation of the assumptions on which it is based.

6 The Product Planning Decision

In this chapter, we discuss some of the more important determinants of the final choice of which new product projects to complete, given the kind of information that is *likely* to be available to the firm at the time it makes the decision. Obviously, once we depart from the optimal situation in which perfect information is available to the firm, so that the standard techniques of investment analysis can be applied to the projects, there will be no one correct method, because different firms will have different kinds of information available to them. We also have to be realistic and not rely on recommendations that it is impossible to come to the right decision unless certain types of information are available. Information-gathering constraints have to be accepted at this stage, even though earlier their validity may have been questioned. Since no one decision-making method will be *right* in this situation, we concentrate here on investigating the logic of decision-making of this kind, in order to facilitate the construction of the appropriate decision-making machinery for firms in different situations.

First, however, in order to bring out the difference between the ideal decision-making environment and the type of decision-making environment that is most common in practice, we outline the requirements for an optimal decision to be made.

As we stated in Chapter 2 an essential requirement for an optimum decision to be made is that the aims of the firm should be known and well-accepted. In addition, if there is conflict of aims, the rate of trade-off between the aims needs to be well-established. A second requirement is that the aims should be quantifiable. For example, 'market domination' is not an aim according to which decisions can be made – it needs to be translated into some combination of sales, market share, profit, etc., aims. Thirdly, if managers making a decision are to be allowed to use their personal judgement in any matter, this needs to be explicitly stated. For example, if higher management has decreed domination of the market as an aim of new product policy, but how this is to be achieved is to be left to individual managers, then this point must be stated and the factors which are assessed as being important according to their judgement have to be explicitly described. For example, managers may rate more highly a product which takes a high market share in one market than a product which, although showing higher profitability and absolute sales, takes a lower market share in its own market.

The information input into the decision should consist of a complete cost and a complete revenue profile (including interest rates) over the life of the product. For each product, the cost profile is assumed to have been arrived at through making a series of assumptions about the production and other characteristics of the product at particular sales levels. The revenue profile is assumed to have been arrived at by establishing, through extensive demand analysis, what price could be charged for each particular level of sales.

The price assumption, although inextricably bound up with the cost analysis, needs to be discussed further here, for the feasibility of obtaining certain price levels, given product, promotion and distribution characteristics, will be bound up with the decision whether to produce the product. In practice, the price decision cannot be made through an optimising process for the same reason that none of the other decisions can : there simply is not enough information available. We discuss the pricing decision in more detail in the following chapter, but some indication of the way in which the price can feasibly be fixed needs to be given here.

The firm, for the purposes of the 'go–no-go' decision, has to fix on a price level to obtain a revenue estimate, even if later on it reappraises this price decision. The major guide will come from the demand analysis, which gives the firm some idea of the relationship between price and sales. In each time period, the firm therefore has information on the relationship between price and sales and between cost and production, both the relationships being very approximate and the latter being based on assumption about feasible sales levels for which cost statistics have been gathered. If we assume that the firm has chosen a fixed number of levels of output to estimate costs, then it has to compare these costs with the revenue obtained by charging the price revealed in the demand analysis as most likely to yield the sales level in question. Then it chooses between the different prices according to the one that leads to the best realisation of its business aims. In principle, this process has to be repeated for every time period, but in practice the firm may be able to distinguish between a few types of time period, perhaps introductory and post-launch.

D

REQUIREMENTS FOR COMPLETE COST–REVENUE PROFILES FOR ALL PRODUCT POSSIBILITIES OVER TIME

In order to bring home the problems involved in using an optimising process, we now summarise the requirements for obtaining a complete cost–revenue profile suited to this.

1. *Revenue profile.* Optimum level of sales (in physical terms) for each time period. (This is defined as the level of sales of the product which most enables the firm to achieve its aim in each time period.)

Optimum price. (The price which best enables the firm to achieve its optimum sales, which in turn will depend upon optimum price. In order to forecast this, the firm needs to be able to forecast not only the demand characteristics of the market, but also the likely development of the competitive situation. Optimum price will also depend upon cost considerations.)

2. *Cost profile.* Optimum level of production in each time period. (This will not necessarily be the same as sales, because of the possibility of holding stocks. It will depend in turn upon unit costs, sales and capacity levels.)

Optimum level of costs in each time period. (Though it may sound strange to put it this way, the existence of several cost variables, such as promotion, which improve the performance of products makes it sensible to refer to the 'optimum' rather than the 'minimum' level of costs. This will depend upon sales, competitive action and interest rates.)

If it can be assumed that the time profile of costs and revenue has been obtained, they then have to be put together. If the aim of the firm is simply to choose the new product project which maximises profits (in the restricted sense that it yields the highest profit out of the alternatives investigated) then the next step is simply to find the amount of profit arising in each time period by subtracting the costs from the sales revenue. Then, taking into account the qualifications discussed in Chapter 2, the firm has simply to discount them according to the appropriate interest rate. This is likely to be a suitable approach for products which make a minor alteration to the firm's uses of resources and to its total profits. But if the product is a major one, then several cautionary points need to be mentioned.

The first point concerns the *most scarce* resources which the firm has used. If the firm has costed all its inputs according to opportunity costs, then any serious limitation will be represented by a high opportunity cost. For example, if it is really impossible to expand the employment of management of a certain quality, and management of that quality is being used in some of the product projects under consideration, then the high valuation which should have been placed on that type of management will be reflected in the high opportunity cost figure attached to them. But suppose, for example, that in addition to this being the case, capital is also plentiful, so that there is little effective limitation on the number of projects that the firm could pursue that arise from the quantity of capital that can be obtained. In this case it is arguable that the profit obtained from the project should be expressed not in relation to the capital input, but rather in relation to the input of the scarcest resource available to the firm, in this case a particular kind of management resource. In this case, the resource should not be included in the calculation at its high opportunity cost. Instead, it should be valued at its money cost, and then the resulting profit figure should be expressed per unit of the resource used. Here, even though we have made simplifying assumptions about the information available to the decision-makers, we are still faced with a major problem concerning the final criterion for the selection of products.

If the firm aims to achieve the highest possible rate of return on capital, what decision rule will enable it to do this, given the assumed resource limitation and the fact that the firm is not considering undertaking just one project, but it will be considering which portfolio of projects is the best? It clearly cannot take up those which yield maximum return on the scarce resource, since these may be low return on capital projects. What it has to do is to establish the level of the resource limitation, pick those projects which maximise profits so that the resource constraint is effective, and then examine whether by deleting any of the projects and adding others, a higher profit combination can be reached. This is a simple process of ranking and substitution.

Perhaps the most important problem here arises from the fact that the figures we are concerned with are multi-period ones. In cases of multi-period constraints which force us to substitute and resubstitute possibilities, we know that the solution has to be arrived at by mathematical programming.[1] But its basic principles remain the same as for the one-period case.

In the case where the firm's aims cannot be represented as simply as profit maximising, further problems arise even in this maximum information case. Suppose, for example, that the firm aims to maximise sales subject to a profit constraint. In this case there will be a fund of profits that needs to be accumulated in each time period, in order to satisfy the profit constraint. The profit constraint will usually take the form not of an absolute amount but rather of a minimum rate of return on capital. This is almost exactly analogous to the scarce-resource situation. Having established the profit, capital usage and sales of each product possibility in each period, the firm uses mathematical programming to establish which combination of products leads to the highest sales while satisfying the profit constraint. There may be problems if in a few periods the profit constraint is not satisfied but may be satisfiable by borrowing from another period. This raises questions about the rationality of such constrained maximisation in a multiperiod analysis. It is unlikely that the firm will be able to forecast precisely its need for a particular level of profit from new product projects, since this will depend on the profit that will be yielded from its on-going activities.

A more sensible view of aims may be that the firm should aim at a portfolio of projects which have different characteristics. These characteristics would include, for example, high risk associated with high profit, high confidence associated with high sales but lower profits, medium profits and medium sales, etc. This view, which is particularly suited to new products analysis, is based on the idea that maximisation of any kind is infeasible, and that the firm's desire for survival is best achieved by having a mixed portfolio. This view has a lot to be said for it, but before adopting it a firm has to be sure that there is no more rational way of setting up its objectives.

THE PRACTICAL SITUATION

As we noted in Chapter 2, the situation in practice is likely to dictate to some extent the aims which are adopted by the firm. Most firms do in practice 'satisfice', and although this type of aim may have some theoretical defects, in that it may in some cases lead to a lower level of performance than might have been obtained otherwise, the quality of the information available to the firm does not allow it to formulate its aims with much element of maximising.

Satisficing aims will normally be phrased in terms of profit and sales level, rates, etc. These may be expressed for each time period or for the whole expected life of the product. The difference between the two is important only if there are adverse consequences of certain distributions over time of the results. We take the simple case of where the aims are expressed for the lives of the products first.

SATISFICING OVER THE LIFE OF THE PRODUCT

We assume here that the firm has only two components of satisficing, rate of return on capital and an average real (price-corrected) sales level. If there are in practice more components, the case differs merely in its complexity rather than in type. A product possibility is deemed acceptable if it passes the test of having a rate of return (as calculated by internal rate of return over the period[2]) of more than $R\%$ and if its average level of sales is more than S per annum. R should be determined by the likely cost of capital. It will not usually be equal to it, because this makes no allowance for the risk of failure (unless this has already been included in the expected profit figures). The rate by which R exceeds the current interest rate on capital borrowings will be determined by the firm's view of the past relation between the projected rate of return on new products and the consequent overall rate of return on the firm's capital when these products have been established. This will usually involve making an unproved generalisation about the behaviour of past and future markets and products, but normally the firm will have no choice about this.

The S will be determined by the firm's view concerning what share of the market for each particular product will be necessary for the product to survive in the long run and what sort of contribution to the firm's overall sales is necessary for the firm to survive in the long run. This too will be a highly subjective matter, and recognised as such by most firms. In fact, because pricing policies often make sales show a strong correlation with profits – stronger than might be expected from the actual economies of selling larger amounts – firms may place more emphasis on the profit figure, knowing that sales are likely to 'come right' if profits do.

The firm should then inspect the rough calculations it has made on the basis of demand and cost estimates to see which products are likely to exceed its requirements. Remembering the likely inaccuracy of its calculations, the firm should now carry out a comprehensive sensitivity analysis on those products which *prima facie* seem likely to satisfy its requirements. It should also re-examine the assumptions it made in arriving at the results for product possibilities which narrowly fail to qualify, to check whether there is much likelihood that the product will qualify, especially in the light of any information received since the appropriate stage.

For each of the rough calculations, an estimate of the likely variation in the stated figure should be made. For example, the capital cost input at the expected sales level should be included as an expected value, a maximum possible value and a minimum possible value. Interdependencies between these maximum and minimum values also need to be taken into account. For example, suppose that there was a certain likelihood that competitive pressure would reduce the level of physical sales and the price received below the expected level. This would also have consequences for the unit costs, which would need to be re-examined. If this competitive pressure persisted, then there might be some possibility of the firm reducing its unit costs by rearranging its equipment set-up.

There will obviously be a strong subjective element in the assessment of maximum and minimum possible values that enter into the calculations. As always, this subjective element must be explicitly recognised. The planning documentation should always contain clear summaries of the areas in which these kinds of assumptions have had to be made, so that the firm can allow for them and so that it knows where to feed-in any extra information that might become available.

For each product possibility, there will be an expected rate of return and sales performance, a minimum and a maximum performance. Having isolated as a group all those products for which the expected performance exceeds the required performance, the firm should then consider whether the distance of the minimum and maximum points from the expected value is such as to affect its attitude to the investment, according to its desired portfolio of risk levels for investments. There may be some products which are considered to be too risky for inclusion in any portfolio, but normally, until the firm has decided upon the major characteristics of its investment portfolio, it cannot *a priori* dismiss a particular possibility.

There are two important factors which will determine how many of the product possibilities which the firm estimates to satisfy its requirements will be actually undertaken. These are the resource question and riskiness (which we have already noted to be associated with each other).

As we mentioned when dealing with the extent to which resource limitations should determine the area of search, the extent to which a product uses the current resource base of the firm is principally important not as an absolute constraint but more as an indicator of risk. It is legitimate to bring this consideration in explicitly at the end of the analysis.

If a product satisfies the satisficing criteria of the firm, how can its resource demands' consistency with the resource base of the firm be measured? There is a wide literature on this topic,[3] but rather than summarise it, we shall try to distil the essence of it.

The first step is to draw up the categories of the firm's resources, which include physical, financial, management and intangible (e.g. goodwill) resources. The idea is that the firm, having listed its resources $R_1 \ldots \ldots R_n$, assigns scores to each resource according to the importance of each sphere of activity in the competitive environment of each product possibility and according to the company's level of competence within each sphere. This raises two important questions, as follows :

(1) How does the firm define a resource?
(2) How does the firm calculate its level of competence?

The problem of resource definition is a serious one. For example, sales force strength and strength of representation in the distribution system are clearly not independent of each other. When the firm comes to evaluate the performance of a new product proposal within a resource sphere (one of the later stages), it may be misleading to score the product separately for the two resources, since the fact that (for example) a new product could be handled well by one resource might not be relevant if it cannot be handled well by the other. This problem might be soluble by a minute sub-division of resources as defined, or else by an explicit statement of interdependence and the appropriate procedure for dealing with it. But both of these raise problems concerning the ability of management to evaluate products in this more complicated way.

The calculation of the firm's level of competence within a resource definition is admitted to be a highly subjective matter. It has to be done separately for each type of competitive environment. For example, a firm's marketing resources may be strong relative to the firms in the market for one of the product possibilities but weak relative to firms in the market for another product possibility. In other words, in evaluating resources, the firm cannot state without any qualification that it is strong in a particular resource.

The actual scoring of the strength of the resources is best done on a simple numerical scale. This is a matter for the subjective decision of management. Take manufacturing capability as an example. The sort of factors which management would be expected to take into account would be the ease with which the firm had set up manufacturing systems for new products in the past, any problems it might have had in all its manufacturing systems, the amount of qualified manpower available to set up the system, and so on. There is bound to be a substantial appeal to past experience here, with all the problems that this brings.

If it is assumed that these various stages can be carried out, the outcome is a resource profile of the firm. The compatibility of each new product possibility with this resource profile now has to be estimated.

The new product possibilities then have to be scrutinised, and a profile of their *requirements* is drawn up, using as definitions the resource categories used for determining the firm's profile. Again, this has to be done by using a simple rating scale within each category. The two rating scales can be brought together in various ways. We do not investigate in detail how this should be done. Rather, we concentrate on the rationale of it.

First, the firm has to decide what its attitude is to a given capability C_n in resource R_n exceeding the product's demands D_n for that resource at different levels of D_n and C_n. Assuming that the resources and product demands are measured on a compatible scale, so that $C_n = D_n$ means that the firm's capability in resource n is equal to the product's demands on it, then it is clear that it may make no difference whether $C_n = D_n$ or $C_n > D_n$ (i.e. the firm's capability in R_n is more than required by the product possibility in question), so long as $C_n \geqslant D_n$. An excess of a resource capability over a demand may not improve the way in which the demand is provided for. It would only be important if $C_n > D_n$ if this actually did lead to a better-than-expected performance.

It should however be noted that the resource inventory is not an inventory of *spare* resources, but of *all* resources. If resources are not being used for the new product, they may be being used for another product. It is too much to expect a firm to compile an inventory of the strengths of spare resources, since this would involve hypothetical releases of resources and measuring the quality of these hypothetical releases, without it being certain how they would be used. It is feasible to measure them only in existing uses. This raises certain problems concerning the extent to which resources can in practice be freed for a new product. This in principle should be taken care of by an opportunity cost analysis.

If, on the other hand, $D_n > C_n$, then this will be significant in most cases, since it will normally lead to a lower level of performance for the product unless resources can be secured. It is at this point that the risk analysis re-enters. Because the firm will have to acquire resources to fill the gap, the problems of resource acquisition and the relation of new resources to performance levels (a calculating problem) will be raised, with the usual problems of indeterminacy caused by lack of information.

One way of scoring in this analysis would be to adopt a standard score for where $C_n \geqslant D_n$, weighted by D_n (an index of the importance of the resource), and to subtract from this standard score some function of $D_n - C_n$, where $D_n > C_n$. This function would be determined partly by D_n (the index of the importance of the resource to the success of the particular product possibility) and partly by an estimate of the difficulty of obtaining the resources to reach the appropriate level of C_n.

In principle, after a process something like this, the product will come out with a score, and the firm will choose those products which, having gone through the rest of the analysis, have the highest score.

This resources-orientated method of making the final elimination of products has to be used very carefully and adapted to the needs of each individual company. But, as we shall see, once we have introduced the time dimension, it becomes a useful check.

SATISFICING WITHIN EACH TIME PERIOD OF THE PRODUCT'S LIFE

The difference between the situation in which the firm has to choose products according to their behaviour in total and the situation in which it has to take into account their performance within individual time periods is a question of the extent to which a firm is willing to *allow* compensation between periods and of the extent to which compensation is *practicable*.

There will normally be some periods in which the targets desired by management are not reached, even if we exclude the case of the introductory period (for which management may set especially low targets). If either the sales or profits dip below the target figures in the forecast, this may be due to special factors. For example, the firm might forecast that in the fifth year competitive pressures would force them to cut the price of the product, thereby reducing the profit yield and the sales revenue. If the product is important to the firm as a source of revenue, then the firm will have to examine whether other products are likely to make good this shortfall and whether, if borrowings are possible (in the case of profits), the product could 'repay' them by earning more than the required level in later years.

This makes the business of product choice even more difficult. For it becomes not simply a question of finding those products which exceed the required levels over their whole life and then choosing between them according to the desired risk structure. Rather, the firm has to find some way of allowing for compensation in its calculations. This it can do only by examining the products as a group and identifying any points at which, say, they all fail to meet the criteria. By doing this, the firm will get a clearer idea of when it will be important if the sales or profit yield is below the required level (this applies only if the new product development programme is a very high proportion of the firm's activity). Compensation will therefore be disallowed during these periods. Again, mathematical programming could be used to impose the constraint that the programme as a whole yield a certain minimum in any one period and a given total over the whole period, thus saving the tedious business of manually switching combinations to see which one produced the best result.

As a final check on the feasibility of the product plan, the firm must align it with the planned development of resources within the firm. We have maintained consistently throughout this book that resources can nearly always be obtained at some cost, whether this be low or high. But the acquisition of resources has always to be planned well in advance. While the firm is considering its product plan, other alterations in policy will be going on which will involve a change in the disposition of the firm's resources. The firm should therefore make an approximate plan of its resource development, paying particular attention to the strengthening or weakening of certain aspects. It should then assess the ease with which it would be possible to integrate any of the product possibilities into this overall development. The firm also needs to consider whether, depending on the extent of resource base change anticipated for the whole firm during the product planning period, a particular resource limitation adopted as a constraint can be relaxed. This also applies to the scoring system discussed above, since the appropriate scoring may change over the life of the product.

THE PRODUCT PLANNING DECISION:
CONCLUSIONS

In this chapter we have not sought to give a definite prescription for the product choice process. Rather, we have been concerned to show what kind of problems are involved in making the final choice of product. General systems of choice have received some discussion, but the responsibility for the details of the system has to rest with the firm, because these depend crucially on the management charateristics of the firm. Product planning must be integrated into the corporate planning of the firm (even if the latter is only an informal process). Even if the firm has very clear ideas about the profit and sales characteristics that it desires from products, these will not be enough to enable it to make the decision (and in this chapter we assumed some of the simplest possible business aims). Quite how this may work in practice we investigate in our worked-out example in Chapter 8.

7 The Marketing and Management of New Products

INTRODUCTION

Once the firm has decided which new product or combination of new products to produce, it is immediately faced with two problems. The first concerns the marketing of the product. Normally, the process of evaluating new products takes long enough for there to be substantial changes in the market while the product is being evaluated. Although the firm has tried to predict these changes in its demand analysis, it is normally sensible, when formulating the marketing plan for the product, to reconsider some of the more important marketing variables, values of which were assumed for the viability analysis. In addition, the fact that the product has reached its final formulation will enable the firm to carry out a more accurate analysis.

The second problem faced by the firm is how to organise the product's management. New products often have fundamentally different characteristics from existing products and may demand different forms of management. But the management system designed for them will have to take over from the system which carried out the evaluation process. We therefore take the opportunity in this chapter to consider the general relationship between management systems and new products, although we place the emphasis on the management of the new product itself rather than on the management of the whole process of product planning.

THE MARKETING OF NEW PRODUCTS

In this section, we concentrate on the problems of fixing the appropriate levels of marketing variables once the product is in production. We do not consider all possible marketing variables, but instead concentrate on the three most important ones, pricing, promotion and distribution.

PRICING

The major problem with the final price fixing is that alterations of prices can have an effect in themselves, such that the firm's freedom to change prices *once the product is launched* may be constrained. The limits on price alteration come not just from Government (although this has become increasingly probable in inflationary situations) but also from the effects of the psychology of buyers. The importance of the buyer's view of price increases will depend upon the general rate of price increase in the economy and the frequency with which a product is bought. In an inflationary situation, it is normally the case that price increases have a less dramatic effect than when prices are stable, even if the real effect is the same. Price reductions, on the other hand, may have a larger effect than in times of steady prices because of buyers' tendencies to search for lower prices. There are also important administrative costs associated with price changes (for example, changing of price lists and promotional publications). On the other hand, the distribution system may take up a lot of the burden of putting the price change into effect. Sales can even be brought forward by promotions at 'pre-increase' prices.

Frequency of purchase is clearly going to affect consumers' perception of price changes. If it is a long time since a given consumer bought the product, he is less likely to remember what it last cost him to buy it. Thus, durable product producers may have to worry less about fixing the price right at the first attempt because of the scope they will have for altering it. Linked to this is the structure of pre-launch ordering. If the product is such that distributors have to be well-stocked with the item before the launch (as with many grocery foods, for example), then the first price chosen will be the one at which a major proportion of the year's sales will be sold. Even if the distributors do not carry large stocks of the item, pre-launch ordering may be at fixed prices.

For these and many other reasons, there may be limits on the extent to which the firm can in practice alter its price. There is therefore a strong incentive to re-examine the price before the launch of the product. All the factors that were included in the final stage of the detailed demand analysis need to be investigated again, and any significant changes noted. For example, if income estimates for the market segment into which the product is going to be launched have been revised downwards, then some consideration may have to be given to dropping the price slightly. But the most important developments are likely to be in competitors' policies. If there is an accepted structure of leadership in the market into which the firm is introducing its product, then alterations in policies by any of the leaders will require appropriate alterations in the marketing plan for the firm's own product. In general, if the firm is introducing its product into a well-established market, a re-examination of the marketing policies of all competitive products will be in order. In particular, the firm will need to re-examine the pricing structure of the market to see if any gaps have opened up or closed.

Depending on the need for secrecy prior to the launch of the product, this will be the stage at which the market testing of prototypes will have to be carried out. Although in this book we have not stressed the importance of test marketing, this being taken as self-evident for some markets, it is evident that the more the firm uses opportunities to estimate sales levels at particular price levels, the clearer will be its ideas concerning what prices it can finally charge. Test marketing, usually for non-durable products, will enter into the analysis from the earlier stages of the demand analysis (through concept testing) and persist until the final stages. Firms should take care to set up any test marketing results such that valid conclusions can be drawn from it. The costs of true test marketing[1] are normally high enough to preclude it until the very latest stages of the analysis.

Changes in costs will also need to be assessed at this final stage. There may be technical changes which have had to be carried out as the design is finalised. These may or may not have added to the product's marketability, but they will normally affect its profitability and hence the appropriate price level. It is only if the firm is in the position of a price taker, with no, or hardly any, room for manoeuvre on the price, that cost changes will have no impact, except through affecting the overall viability of the product.

In markets where the product has to pass through third-party distribution systems, valuable information may by this stage have been received about distributors' likely reaction to the proposed price level. If it is considered too high, this does not mean that the price has to be lowered, since distributors themselves may have an inadequate idea of the price that is obtainable for the new product, particularly if it is significantly different from other products on the market. The importance of securing distributive outlets may force a firm to respond to suggestions of revised pricing, but some case for at least an experimental period should be made out.

Finally, as an aid to pricing revisions, management should keep chartered the price and (where possible) sales of competing products. Unless the firm is able to carve out a relatively secure niche for itself in the market, there will always be the risk of a price gap opening up.

Over the life of the product, management will need to examine the behaviour of the market, perhaps using some of the notions employed in the theory of the product life cycle. In particular, it will need to establish the extent to which the price it was able to obtain in the initial period of the product's life was due to any innovatory characteristics it might have had, and whether these characteristics remain innovatory (in the sense that saturation level is not reached) or whether other products surpass its characteristics. In particular, management needs to assess the extent to which any changes that occur are permanent or whether they are merely due to underlying changes in the economy. The answers to these questions will have crucial implications for the firm's pricing policy. For example, if profit margins begin to be squeezed, the firm should not immediately consider reducing marketing expenditure and the price in order to maintain sales, without examining the state of the economy as a whole.

PROMOTION

The determination of promotional levels has always raised problems for management, simply because of the difficulties of establishing the consequences of any given level of promotion. When a product is established on the market and its sale is proceeding at a steady rate or enough data have been gathered for the firm to determine the principal determinants of its rate of sale, the consequences of changes in the level of promotion may be established relatively easily. But for a new product, this raises difficulties. It is only if the new product resembles some existing products in its price, design and distributional characteristics that the firm will be able to decide without too many problems what level of promotion will be necessary.

The trouble with using practices for existing products as a justification for assuming that a particular level of promotion will be necessary to obtain a particular level of sales is that the promotional levels for existing products will often be determined on the same grounds. For example, a particular percentage of revenue might always have been spent on promoting a product and, a firm might argue, since the majority of products promoted with this proportion had proved to be successful, therefore this proportion should be adopted for any future products. In this case, given the almost certain existence of economies of scale in promotion, it is unlikely that a constant proportion of sales revenue would be needed, unless it could be shown that as the market grows beyond a certain size successive units become more difficult to sell. This may well be the case, since as the firm's sales grow beyond a certain size, it is more likely to come across competitive resistance. But this is unlikely to be at the same sales level for each product.

Following previous practices is obviously a policy of the last resort. If the firm has made any reasonable attempt at all at demand analysis of the kind discussed in Chapter 3, it should have a fair idea of the response of consumers to promotional variables in physical terms. Therefore the firm should decide what kind of policies are necessary to achieve particular sales levels, and then proceed to cost them. If the cost level proves to be too high to yield the firm the required level of profit, then some experimentation may be possible. Fortunately, promotional variables are normally much more flexible than pricing variables, and thus experimentation is normally possible. However, the firm should always be careful, when making experiments of this kind, to standardise the conditions of the experiment such that results are not incorrectly ascribed. This applies specifically to correction for the effects of competitive action and distributors' policies, which may sometimes negate the effect of promotion.

One final point needs to be covered in the context of promotion. For any product, there will normally be several possible promotional methods that can be used, ranging from television advertising to leafleting (in the case of consumer products) and from exhibitions to in-factory trials (in the case of industrial products). These methods can be substituted for each other according to the needs of the situation. Firms should not adhere rigidly to a particular combination of methods, but should always consider the possibility of switching between them. Certain measures of the effectiveness of different modes of promotion are available (such as readership figures, television audience coverage), but only under special assumptions (for example, that time of exposure is equivalent or at least proportional to effect) are the measures translatable from one medium to another. Firms may find it worth while to try to evolve their own specific equivalence measures, since these would save considerable time and debate when deciding on promotional policy and would be more easily attainable than general equivalence measures.

DISTRIBUTION

Deciding on methods of distribution has many characteristics in common with deciding upon methods of promotion, with one crucial difference, which is that, unless the firm is effectively its own distributor, it has to deal with an independent third (and sometimes a fourth) party before it can reach the final buyer. This situation can completely transform the nature of the relationship between the firm and its market.

The complex relationship between the manufacturer and the distributor is summarised in Fig. 7.1. From this diagrammatic summary of the relationship, we can see that the distributor is an important element to be taken into account at almost every stage of the analysis. The distributor will transform the spacing of demand over time, whether the demand is actually allowed through to the manufacturer, the promotional facilities allowed to confront the buyer at the point of purchase, and so on.

Since the distributor is an independent party to the action, with his own aims to pursue, his actions also need to be predicted. By predicting his actions is meant not just his reaction to the particular new products being marketed by the firm but also any general developments in the field of distribution which would affect his reception of the products. If the firm is already involved in the area in which it is marketing a new product, it will have two advantages. First of all, it will be known to distributors in that area as a producer of products which have had

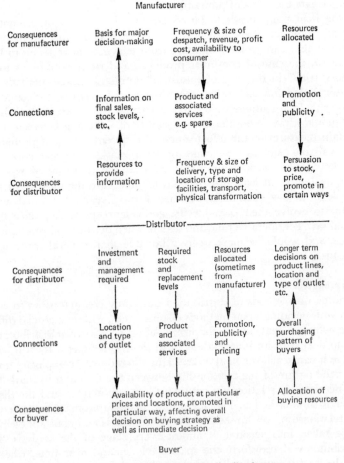

Fig; 7.1 Relationships in a simple distributive system

some success (or at least this will normally be the case, since if the opposite is true, further involvement in the same area can lead to distributor problems). Secondly, it will know a certain amount about the kind of considerations which led to ready adoption of products in the past and about the personal preferences (if any) of the managers of distribution firms. This set of advantages can be one of the most important reasons why firms do prefer to constrain themselves to launching new products in areas with which they are already familiar.

Although the firm new into the market faces extra problems because of distributional factors, it may also possess some advantages. First of all, because it is new, it is more able to assess alternative ways of distributing the product. Quite noticeable changes take place in the ways in which products are distributed. For example, in the U.K. there has been a significant move away from selling technically complex durable products through specialist distributors into selling them through general merchandise stores. It has been noticeable that firms in the forefront of this move have been those who are newer into the market (in this case often importers). This raises an important general point. Just as current promotional methods may be adhered to through inertia in management, so may distributional methods. From its knowledge of the demand characteristics which each product is intended to satisfy, the firm should 'construct' theoretically the ideal distribution system for the product, and *then* search current distribution set-ups for those that best approximate to the ideal. If the firm is strong enough, it might also attempt to change some of the characteristics of the distribution systems that it chooses to make them more suitable to its product.

The most important criterion for choice of distribution system, given the constraint that the distribution system chosen must have the appropriate coverage, is cost. Apart from transport costs, which are in a sense an internal production item (unless affected by external contracts), the principal component of distribution costs is the distributive margin. However, the days in which manufacturers could fix the price for final buyers and then negotiate over the distributive margin are past for most products and never existed for others.[2] But the manufacturer does have some choice over distributive margin because he has choice between different kinds of outlet which typically sell at different margins. Each type of outlet will have different promotional costs attached to it, as well as different price possibilities. For this reason, the three sets of decisions need in the end to be considered together. The price range chosen needs to be consistent with the type of promotion and distribution chosen for the product.

Remembering that it may not be the aim of the firm to get as much profit as possible out of each product, the firm needs to bear constantly in mind the objectives that were specified for the product at the beginning of the analysis, and to analyse market developments for their effect on these objectives. If the firm's aim is first to secure a dominating sales position, then fluctuations in distributional costs may not demand any change in policy. If the firm aimed to achieve a very high level of profit, then changes in the market share may be of less significance than changes in cost.

IMPORTANCE OF THE INFORMATION SYSTEM
Possibly the most crucial requirement for the successful marketing of a new product, especially if the product is significantly different from the existing products of the firm or if the firm does not regularly market new products, is the setting up of an adequate information system to monitor changes in markets. Such an information system must cover at least the following variables :

Prices of competing products (including promotional discounts, special discounts to distributors, etc.);
Promotion of competing products (amount, structure, detailed characteristics);
Distribution of competing products (firms used, breadth of coverage, special advantages gained);
General market characteristics (income, structure of the buying population, tastes, expenditure patterns, etc.);
Technical developments (research output, developments in more advanced markets, etc.).

The firm must also monitor developments on the cost side. Until an adequate information flow becomes available to the firm, marketing is reduced to the level of guesswork.

MARKETING OF GOODS AND MARKETING OF SERVICES
Before turning to the management question, we need to consider whether there are any important differences in principle between the marketing of goods and the marketing of services. First, we need to define the difference between the two.

Though the two terms are easy to use, the distinction between them is a hazy one. When a buyer buys a physical good, he is not buying just a lump of matter, but rather what economists call a 'bundle of satisfactions', which derive their value from the services performed by the product. In a sense, the buyer is the provider of some of the service element in the good, because he is administering the good to himself. This analogy becomes clear when we examine durable products, many of which can either be hired (car hire as opposed to car purchase) or can be used by another agent who is paid for doing the servicing (laundries as opposed to the purchase of a washing machine). The difference between the two is made even more hazy by the fact that many goods are supplied with a service (whether it be a repair guarantee, installation or method of payment). Further, manufacturers, by their promotional methods, often so influence the way in which the product is bought and used that this can be considered to change the good from a simple physical entity into a complex mixture of a good and a service.

There does however remain a difference of degree. A service, when it is bought for the first time, does not usually reveal its quality until after the purchase, whereas the quality of a new good is slightly more 'transparent' to the intending buyer. Sometimes, where the service is very closely specified, as in the conditions of some financial services, the buyer may be able to judge fairly accurately what he is getting, but usually this is not the case. New services therefore should be approached in a slightly different way.

First of all, statistics for market analysis are much more difficult to obtain for services. There is no such thing as factory deliveries. Distribution is most often done by the provider of the service and therefore statistics are not normally publicly available, whereas usually the distributor is the key source of information for manufactured goods, since he has less cause to worry about confidentiality. All this means that forecasting the market in any detail raises tremendous problems. This is exacerbated for new services, the details of which may have to be hypothesised. New products are usually susceptible to market testing, while new services are often not. Although new services may sometimes be made easier by the fact that their production requires less investment, this is not always the case. Extensive promotional outlays may have to be undertaken to inform consumers of the availability of services, while new products often advertise themselves more easily through their use.

The general problem with the marketing of services is that the buyer's reaction is more difficult to obtain. Because the buyer is not so sure of the quality of a service before he buys it, price may be used by him as an index of quality. This makes pricing a particularly difficult problem, since the firm has to balance very carefully the advantages and disadvantages of low or high price levels in terms of judgements on quality and competitive effect. On the other hand, if different people use different levels of price as a criterion of quality, it is often more easy to segment the market for marketing policy purposes. This is because constructive use of any market segmentation analysis[3] is partly dependent on the closeness of contact between buyer and seller. As this is normally closer with services than products, the firm is more able to fix prices according to the customer. This can be a very important advantage, because it enables the firm to alter its prices more quickly in response to any change in cost or market conditions. The same will normally apply to most other marketing variables.

CONSUMER, INDUSTRIAL AND PUBLIC SERVICE MARKETS

Conventionally, considerable stress is laid upon the marketing differences between industrial and consumer products.[4] The research that was undertaken for this book seemed to indicate that the similarities between the two were most striking than the differences. The most important way in which consumer and industrial markets are supposed to differ from each other is in the motivations of buyers. Since public service bodies are now in many economies at least as important buyers as industrial buyers, it seems sensible to introduce them as a separate category, since their purchasing motivations are clearly different from either of the other two. The industrial buyer is conventionally represented as buying only when it can be demonstrated that the product produces a beneficial effect on expected rate of return, while the consumer buys for his personal satisfaction or that of his family. The public-service buyer has always been a slight misfit in the marketing scene, because it is known that the way in which estimates are set up leads to very inflexible behaviour, and produces a need for the firm with a product or service to sell to dig very deep into the organisation of the potential buyer in order to find out what point it is appropriate to try and introduce the product idea.

Many firms, especially the larger ones, now show buying characteristics that are very similar to public corporations. Take for example office equipment provision. Instead of deciding on any optimum level of service, taking cost considerations into account, many firms simply state requirements irrespective of cost and then leave it to the appropriate manager to make sure that these requirements are met (the same applies to many of the service requirements of firms, such as transport). The manager then may take estimates on costs and buy the equipment which seems to show the best balance between cost and service level, just as the public-service manager, when he is told of a decision made higher up (often by the political authorities), then has to find the cheapest way of supplying a particular service. Alternatively, the procedure may be to allocate a particular sum to a particular category of expenditure, on the basis of approximate estimates, and then leave it to the individual manager to sort out the policy from that point.

There are also similarities between the firm, the public authority and the consumer, because managers to whom decisions are delegated are often allowed to choose on a more or less personal basis. In this case, factors like the desire to purchase from sources with which the buyer is well acquainted can be important. Inertia, the desire to continue in old patterns of behaviour, is a clear impediment here to the marketing of new products.

The marketing of new products to industrial buyers clearly needs to be orientated towards these three aspects of industrial buying: namely, the extent to which the product can help to satisfy the explicit aims of the firm (usually profitability, as far as input purchasing is concerned), the extent to which it is easy for the manager making the purchase to order the product (e.g. making it easy for him to persuade superiors, introducing some personal satisfactions for him into the purchase, etc.) and the extent to which the product/promotion/pricing package attracts the attention of the firm. In a similar way, the marketing of new products to the other two buyers should pay attention to the convenionally unstressed aspects of the purchasing decision (for example, treating the family as a buying organisation).

THE MANAGEMENT OF NEW PRODUCTS

In this section, the influence of organisational factors on new product policy is investigated. Rather than attempting to produce a comprehensive analysis, which space considerations do not allow, the concern of this section is to bring out certain points which are of great importance to the firm considering the organisation of its new product policy.

There are several important factors which will affect the kind of organisation system which will be most suited to the needs of the firm. They include the following:

(*a*) the size of the firm or of the appropriate decision-making unit (e.g. department or division) within the firm;
(*b*) The kind of contact required with customers, suppliers and with other parts of the firm;
(*c*) The kind of technology embodied in the design and manufacture of the new product;
(*d*) The speed with which the product has to be produced and launched for it to succeed;
(*e*) The market position of the firm;
(*f*) The characteristics of the organisation of the other parts of the firm.

There are various dimensions along which an organisation can vary to suit these types of requirement. First of all, there is the distinction between how the organisation is formally structured and how informal relationships are set up within the firm. Secondly, there is the distinction between how the organisation is formally structured (i.e. what it looks like if summarised on an organisation chart) and the actual process of evaluation which new product ideas have to undergo. Then there are some more basic categories, as follows :

> The number of levels in an organisation;
> The span of control of members of the organisation;
> The type of control of members (vetting, etc.);
> The type of relationship between members (information, etc.);
> The quality of staff at different levels;
> The conditions of work at different levels;
> Level of remuneration at different levels;
> The flexibility of the organisation (e.g. ease of transfer of resources between areas with different responsibilities);
> The type of division of responsibility.

Within these categories, there are certain areas which have received particular attention, for example, the division between organisations which are set up along functional lines (e.g. with marketing, finance, sales and production departments) and organisations which are based broadly on product groupings (which have various variations, from the idea of product management through to that of venture management).

Although various studies have been carried out to try to prove the superiority of particular systems,[5] their validity is always in question for particular firms. We shall try, however, to give some general indications of how systems might be designed, by considering in turn the factors listed at the beginning of this section.

THE SIZE OF THE FIRM OR DECISION-MAKING UNIT

The larger the firm, the greater the problems of communication over policy, other things being equal. However, if adequate thought is given to the problem of communication, the outcome in a large firm can be better than in a small concern which considers the problem insignificant and so fails to devote enough attention to it. Problems of responsibility and motivation are also generally commoner in the small firm. Both these problems arise normally because, given the need for some control and given the fact that one manager can effectively control only a limited number of subordinates, the number of levels of organisation normally necessary is greater in the larger firm. There are several ways of overcoming these problems of size. The normal way is by splitting the firm up into appropriate departments, but it is not always clear what 'appropriate' means in this context. It is here, in the larger firm, that the distinction between functional and product management is considered to be most appropriate. If the procedure for the evaluation of new product possibilities involves many departments, then there is a possibility that no one manager will see it as his brief to take products through from their earliest stages to success as a product in sale. For this reason, product managers are sometimes appointed,[6] such that even if the firm remains organised along functional lines, there will be at least some responsibility for the individual product that cuts across these lines of organisation. If firms commit themselves completely to product management, with the work of product development departments being taken over at the appropriate stage by the product departments themselves, then the opposite risk is that overall responsibility for finance, marketing, etc. tends to become slightly lost. In fact, the best answer is usually some compromise between the two, with responsibility for major areas continuing along functional lines (only being split up if the firm is so large that product units can economically be treated as separate units) with a considerable element of product responsibility cutting across it, so that the firm does not lose the advantages of managers being specialised in single products with the right to approach management at considerably higher levels on policy matters. A more extreme form of product management, namely *venture management*, is sometimes used in an attempt to compensate for some of the disadvantages of size. Recognising that in the large firm there may not be the drive amongst the managers actually concerned with a product to push the product as far as it will go, some firms try to recreate the conditions of a small firm by giving a team complete financial and marketing responsibility for a particular product's development and marketing. This type of experiment has, paradoxically, to be controlled very strictly. The terms of reference of the system have to be made very clear, for unless the managers in the team are actually personally involved in the financing of the product, the conditions of the smaller firm are not closely approximated, and risks may be taken which the smaller firm would not take.

The flexibility of a firm does not necessarily diminish with its size, and in fact may increase with the possibilities of spreading risk. As has been repeatedly stressed, it is crucial for the firm's attitude towards the use of resources and towards product ranges to be a flexible one. One of the disadvantages of product management is that it can lead to an inflexibility over product ranges which would not be produced in a functional organisation. For this reason, new product research and development departments and broadly briefed market research departments are essential to the firm, whatever its form of organisation but particularly when it is organised along product lines.

CONTACT WITH CUSTOMERS, SUPPLIERS AND OTHER PARTS OF THE FIRM

The important difference between new products and existing products as far as this topic goes lies in the non-routine nature of much of the activity. Communication of routine information can be carried out well enough in most systems of management, but once the information begins to concern non-routine subjects, it begins to become difficult to express and communicate in such a way that the manager conveying it can be certain that it is understood. For this reason, more time usually has to be spent on this kind of information, such that organisation dealing with it can probably do so more effectively if the span of control of each manager is narrower. Because of the complexity of the information conveyed, assessment will take longer, so it may be important, if the firm is continually dealing with new products, to streamline the vetting procedure. New product development usually requires closer contact with the customer than day-to-day marketing, and here the flexibility of the organisation can be important in allowing individual managers some independence in developing links outside the firm in order to maintain the close relationship necessary for accurate estimation of demand for new products.

Close contact with customers is most important in demand areas where formal market research is costly or infeasible. In such cases, particular stress needs to be laid upon easing the information flow between parts of the organisation that are in contact with potential customers and those that are concerned with product planning. Given the stress which in this book has been laid on the importance of considering possibilities not closely related to the mainstream of the firm's activities, it is suggested here that some attention be given to the flow of information on these possibilities. Members of the firm are constantly coming into contact with markets outside the mainstream of the firm's activities, and should be encouraged to use the information they obtain from these markets in helping to decide the appropriate direction of product policy.

TECHNOLOGY EMBODIED IN THE DESIGN AND MANUFACTURE OF THE NEW PRODUCTS

There has been a certain amount of debate concerning the general type of organisation suitable for different manufacturing systems.[7] In particular, the difference between mass-produced and other products has received considerable attention, some writers maintaining that it is more appropriate for mass production to be accompanied by more rigid forms of organisation. But what concerns us here is the way in which the problem is relevant to new products. Whatever form of organisation a firm has found to be most appropriate for its existing products, some other form may be more appropriate for its new products if they involve a different technology of production. For example, if the firm is used to producing very long production runs of a standard commodity, and marketing analysis shows that it would be worth while to introduce some element of differentiation or even custom-building, then this will clearly demand some change in its management methods. This will probably involve introducing some flexibility into the organisation to make it responsive to changes in the best ways of differentiating products, etc.

The management of the design of new products is a crucial point. The closeness of the relationship between design staff and other staff, particularly marketing and production, is an important determinant of the produceability and marketability of a new product. The way in which design staff are integrated into the organisation of the firm, in particular the extent to which they are allowed to derive their own satisfactions from the design process, can have a substantial impact on the output of a design department.

THE SPEED WITH WHICH THE PRODUCT HAS TO BE PRODUCED AND LAUNCHED FOR IT TO SUCCEED

The speed which a firm requires from its decision-making cannot be produced automatically. Critical path analysis and other similar techniques have been devised to help firms with a given form of organisation achieve results within specified times by isolating critical points in the process of policy change. These same methods can be used in the longer term to devise systems which are suited to the requirements of product planning. The major problem here is that the times required for the different steps in the product-planning process are extremely uncertain. However, even if simultaneous planning techniques cannot be used, the firm can at least work out which steps of the product-planning process can be carried out simultaneously. For example, it is clear that if the firm follows some of the procedures recommended in this book, there will be a continuous to-ing and fro-ing between the development and the marketing teams as the marketing department finalise their estimates of the most-demanded product characteristics and the development team work out the feasibilities. The way in which the firm is organised should be such as to make this interaction possible at a high speed. It may be useful not to define responsibilities too closely between development and marketing in order that managers can be involved in both sides of the question.

THE MARKET POSITION OF THE FIRM

The extent to which the firm has control over the market in which it is launching a new product will principally have its effect through the need for flexibility. A firm which has very few competitors does not need to waste its organisational resources in making sure that it is capable of responding to changes in the market. The long-run position may be different, but in general the firm will do better to concentrate its resources where it is most at risk, depending on its business aims. This applies to the quality of staff and level of remuneration as well.

Although this seems to suggest a relatively short-term view, that the firm should place its best resources where it is likely to be 'under attack', this view is not really so extreme. Basically, the idea is that the firm should actively consider in what market area among its new products it most needs higher quality management, instead of assuming that it needs the same quality throughout the firm.

THE CHARACTERISTICS OF THE ORGANISATION OF OTHER PARTS OF THE FIRM

One of the constantly recurring problems in the management of new products is that, because they involve the integration of activities over a number of departments in the firm and because these departments may be organised in different ways, communication between the departments may in practice be hindered by the fact that managers from one department who would like another department to take a particular action do not know how best to obtain that action because they are not used to dealing with the relationships involved. An additional problem may be that because of the difficulties that communication between members of different departments has caused in the past (in terms of heads of departments not knowing precisely what their departments are doing) the firm has decided that all communication between departments shall be at a relatively senior level. But product planning, of its very nature, requires rapid communication between members of many departments at various levels of seniority. Therefore some way must be found to facilitate this communication without destroying the basic management structure. One way of doing this, as we have seen, is to set up cross-departmental responsibilities, but in certain circumstances the same aim may be achieved by a well-thought-out reporting system.

If the firm is considering separate organisation of product responsibility, it should consider the point that the kind of hierarchy in use elsewhere in the firm is not necessarily the best for organising product responsibilities. Different kinds of new products will, as we have suggested, demand different kinds of organisation, but the firm should not simply transpose or adapt its current structure, without considering the needs of each product.

THE MARKETING AND ORGANISATION OF NEW PRODUCTS: FINAL POINTS

To what extent can the firm *plan* to cope with the marketing and organisation of its new products? Firms obviously do set up marketing plans for new products, but these often get lost in the problems of day-to-day management and in the welter of changes that occur in the market and that outdate any of the decisions made at the time of the launch. What is really needed is a contingency plan, based on the objectives for the product. Marketing indicators need to be selected which will give the firm information on the extent to which its aims are being met. The firm should plan to monitor these continuously and should prepare contingency plans (which in their turn need to be undated) for the most important possibilities that might arise.

Probably more dividends are to be had from planning the *organisation* of new products, however, since this is something which is nearly always neglected. The problem is that the kind of organisation that suits one new product will not necessarily suit another, so that instead of considering just one new system for the organisation of new products, firms should consider, as suggested here, the different dimensions of new products and what kind of organisation they will require. A firm might consider it worth while setting up an 'organisational contingency plan' which allows for the different categories of new products and for the development of these characteristics over time.

8 Conclusions

INTRODUCTION

Throughout this book, the main theme has been that each aspect of product policy only makes sense if it is considered together with all other aspects of product policy. Thus, for example, search for product possibilities cannot be considered in isolation from market possibilities and business aims, while organisational aspects must be considered in conjunction with marketing aspects. However, it is sometimes difficult to represent these points to the reader in a way that brings them home. This can sometimes be done with the use of examples scattered throughout the text, but the problem with this is that by the time the reader reaches the end of the book, he may have lost the thread of thought. For this reason, we have chosen to bring the conclusions together by presenting a worked-through analytical case history of a firm in a particular situation facing the problem of product line change. The example is based on the characteristics of the firms examined for the purposes of the book and the types of market situation encountered. Although it proved impossible to design an example which brings up all the points considered by this book it is hoped that it will answer most of the questions that might arise concerning the viability of the integrated approach. First we summarise the conclusions reached throughout the book, and then proceed with the case history.

The problem with the case history approach is that there is always, for reasons of brevity, the chance that some relevant information will be left out. This is a chance we have to take.

CONCLUSIONS SO FAR

In Chapter 2, the priority of clearly establishing the firm's business aims was stressed. The problems inherent in conventional notions of maximisation were brought out and the conclusion reached that the best that the firm could do was to employ some kind of satisficing procedure, whether just to profits or to other variables as well. The close relation between aims and constraints was singled out as being worth further consideration. Constraints that the firm imposes upon itself or considers to be imposed upon it by the business environment form an important part of planning procedures and sometimes are not given the attention that they deserve.

In Chapter 3, the view was taken that the firm should not impose too many constraints on the area it chooses for future product policy changes. This means in turn that it must devote a lot of resources to the analysis of demand. Although in the end some constraints have to be accepted in a more or less arbitrary fashion, a broad analysis of demand will enable the firm to appreciate the significance of these constraints. This analysis can only be practically carried out in a succession of stages, in each of which further restrictions are imposed on the scope of the analysis.

In Chapter 4, the status of product life cycle analysis was questioned, in an attempt to put into context the problems that arise in some kinds of demand analysis. The points raised in this chapter showed how important it is that the terms used in any demand analysis be closely defined.

In Chapter 5, the problems of deciding upon product specifications and costing them, given the output of the demand analysis, were discussed. The interdependence of the various factors involved means that in essence the firm must try to reserve some of its cost decisions (those which are scale-dependent in particular) until the decisions on the overall viability of the product. But it is recognised that there is bound to be some arbitrariness in some elements of the cost decision.

The difficulties inherent in making a final decision on which products to produce were discussed in Chapter 6. Given the multi-period nature of the decision and the fact that some of the inputs into the decision cannot be determined independently, the firm cannot sensibly make cast-iron decisions on which products to produce without allowing for the possibility of changing them or changing the way in which the product is produced. In addition, some constraints which were to some extent avoidable in the early stage of the analysis may have to be accepted here.

Some indication of the relationship between the product decision, marketing policy and organisational questions was given in Chapter 7. Given the complexity of the interrelations between the product decision and marketing policy, the firm needs to bear in mind the marketing implications of each step of the analysis, from the choice of broad market areas for further investigation to the final product decision. Marketing decisions have to be taken implicitly all along the line, and are subject to the same informational problems as the product decision. This makes it all the more important that the firm should be aware of the consequences of any constraints that it imposes upon itself. As far as organisational considerations are concerned, many of the same points can be made. A common fault is insufficient consideration of the implications of particular types of new product for the organisation of the firm. This can be remedied by introducing organisational variables into the planning procedure at the earliest possible stage.

The picture that emerges from the analysis is that product-planning decisions are very far from being simple marketing planning and investment decisions. In principle, they involve a re-examination of the whole basis of the firm's operations. To the extent that this is infeasible, the firm runs the risk of its decisions producing results that are inconsistent with the firm's aims.

THE CASE OF INTEGRATED PRODUCTS LTD

THE FIRM

Integrated Products Ltd (a publicly quoted company) is a firm which currently (Year 0 of the analysis) employs 3000 workers and had a turnover of £40m per annum in Year -1 (last year). Last year it had capital employed of £20m and made gross profits of £4m (before tax and depreciation). Depreciation amounted to £500,000, while taxation amounted to £1·3m, leaving the firm with a net profit of £2·2m, or 11% on capital. Overall figures for the previous five years are as follows (figures in £000's):

Years	-6	-5	-4	-3	-2
Sales	30,000	33,000	39,000	41,000	39,000
Capital employed	15,000	18,000	20,000	20,000	19,000
Gross profit	1,900	1,800	2,500	3,500	4,100
Depreciation	300	350	450	500	450
Taxation	500	600	800	1,100	1,100
Net profit	1,100	850	1,250	1,900	2,550
Rate of return on capital, net	7·3%	4·7%	6·3%	9·5%	13·4%
Employment (000's)	2·1	2·3	2·4	2·7	2·9

The firm is principally engaged in the supply of small kitchen utensils, gardening equipment and do-it-yourself aids, mainly using the following materials and processes : plastics (various moulding processes), wood (machine-cut to shape), stainless steel (bought-in ready-shaped) and non-ferrous metals, principally aluminium (stamped and drawn).

Integrated Products is organised mainly on functional lines. There is a production department, a marketing department, a finance department and a design and development department.

In year -3, the directors considered the possibility of reorganising

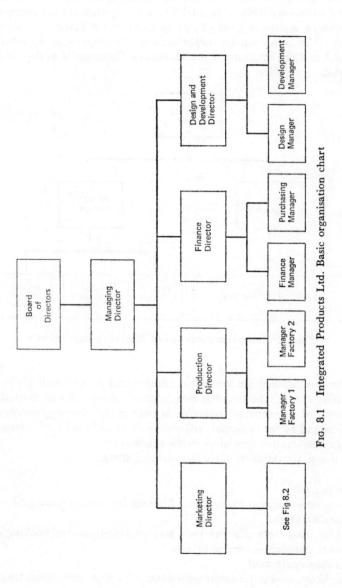

Fig. 8.1 Integrated Products Ltd. Basic organisation chart

the firm along product lines, but the products of the firm were considered to be too closely integrated for such a separation to be profitable. However, a system of product management on the marketing side was set up. The firm's current organisational structure is as depicted in Fig. 8.1 and the structure of the Marketing Department as depicted in Fig. 8.2.

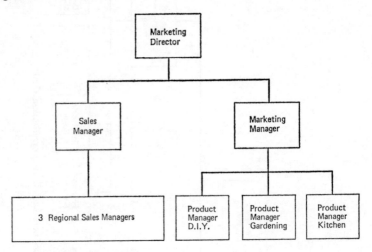

Fɪɢ. 8.2   Integrated Products Ltd. Marketing Department

The two factories are located in London and in the South Midlands (60 miles apart). The firm has two factories because it was created by a merger of two separate concerns in year −15. The headquarters of the firm and all the principal staff are on the site of the London factory. The London factory specialises in the plastics side.

In detail, the products of the firm are as follows.

Do-it-yourself
Various non-precision tools, plastic fitments for various household uses.
Kitchen utensils
Moulded plastic utensils (strainers, etc), part-stainless-steel cooking implements, aluminium saucepans, etc.
Gardening equipment
Plastic hoses, steel implements with wooden handles, aluminium frames.

The contribution to sales of the three major product groups has been as follows :

Years	−6	−5	−4	−3	−2	−1
D.I.Y.	6·1	7·5	9·7	11·9	14·7	18·9
Garden	16·6	17·1	21·1	20·1	18·1	18·0
Kitchen	7·3	8·4	8·2	9·0	6·2	3·1

(All figures are in £m.)

Inflation has been running at a fairly steady average rate, both throughout the economy and in the markets for the firm's products, at around 3%, while the rate of growth of the U.K. G.N.P. has averaged 2·5% over the six years for which the figures are presented. This gives an inflation over the five years between years −6 and −1 of about 16%, so the real increase in sales is about $14\frac{1}{2}$% over the period, while G.N.P. has gone up by just over 13% in the period. However, net profits have increased by 100% in money terms over the period, while capital employed has only increased by 27% in money terms.

ANALYSIS OF PAST RESULTS AND SUGGESTIONS FOR FUTURE STRATEGY
The Board of Directors met in the middle of year 0, when the results for year −1 were published, to consider future strategic developments, in the light of a memorandum by the Managing Director, who had been in his post over the previous eight years. The principal content of the memorandum was as follows :

The company has considerably outperformed the policy laid down by the Board of Directors in year −6, when we began our investment programme, of a minimum net rate of return on capital of 8%. However, this aim was laid down when our borrowing costs for capital investment were running at around 5%. Since then, borrowing costs have risen to 10%, and although this has not affected us severely, since our net borrowing in the recent past has been low, it may have a severe effect in the future.

The strength of the firm's performance has been principally due to the marked boom in do-it-yourself products, supported by some improvement in the market for garden products. These markets have helped us to more than offset the situation which resulted in the kitchen products market following the advent of cheap competitive products on a very large scale from abroad. Although products in the other two markets could be subject to the same competition, because they are made from the same materials and marketed in basically the same way, the distinctive nature of the British market has so far protected us. However, the signs are that the foreign competition is beginning to take an active interest in these markets as well. We consider that our deep knowledge of

E

the U.K. market together with our continuing product development programme for products very closely related to the ones in our current range will give us some protection from this competition, while the quality of our products, which is not matched by foreign competition, will also help us to maintain our share of the market. Nevertheless, the fact remains that our main markets are under threat from foreign competition, not to mention the possibility of developments from our British competition. We therefore need to rethink our strategy and product policy.

The Board of Directors accepted the Managing Director's report, and then started to consider, in a series of meetings, the best course for development.

First, the basic aims of the firm were restated explicitly. The prime requirement was taken to be continuing independence. Given the size of the firm and particularly its current market valuation which, though good relative to the actual outlay on capital, was small enough to make it a takeover prospect for a larger firm seeking to diversify, it was considered by the Board to be possible that this would happen. The firm would therefore have to seek to expand its capital base to make this more difficult. Given the current rate of interest, and the suggested likelihood that it would remain the same or even go higher, this could only be done if more profitable products were found. It was considered that the minimum net rate of return on capital that would be acceptable if the market were to maintain its high valuation of the firm was the current rate in year -1, i.e. 11%, plus any increase in the interest rate on borrowing. The Board considered that it would be reasonable to plan for a doubling in real sales over a ten-year period to allow for the appropriate expansion in the capital base.

The Board took the view that it could not afford to restrict consideration of new products and markets to those areas in which it was currently involved, because of the risk to the firm's current activities from foreign competition. The Board therefore decided that it would be appropriate to undertake a complete re-evaluation of the firm's product policy in order to allow for the widest possible search.

The key question which the Board had to decide was that of the allocation of resources to this search. Most of the product design and development staff were preoccupied either in producing more sophisticated variants of products already on the market in order to avoid the basic competition coming in from abroad, or in designing the production equipment for them. The firm therefore considered it advisable to set up a special *strategic evaluation team*. In order to avoid any problems that might have occurred through failures in communication, the team included members from the most important departments. The Marketing Director was given responsibility for the team's work, and he immediately proceeded to hire another manager from outside with considerable experience of marketing research and quantitative studies.

THE DELIMITATION STAGE

The first step to be taken was that of delimiting the area for intensive demand research. Given the firm's current quite strong financial position and the assumption that this would enable it to raise finance for most moves that it would want to consider, the Marketing Director did not consider it appropriate to impose any *a priori* limitation on the area to be researched. The first step that had to be made was to decide on the relative merits of home and export markets. Here the firm concluded that as far as its existing products were concerned, foreign competition was likely to be just as dangerous abroad as at home, while their trade contacts discovered that the more advanced products that they were trying to bring out in their own area were matched by more advanced products produced by other foreign firms. So it seemed unlikely *a priori* that there would be any more opportunity abroad than at home. As far as export of other products was concerned, it was concluded that there was no point in considering this until the home market for other products had been considered. It was held that, although it was not always necessary for a strong home market to back up an export market, this was normally the case. The firm then turned to further consideration of the home market.

Initially, the team carried out a quick survey, on the basis of published family budget studies, of the extent to which several general categories of expenditure responded to changes in income (i.e. their income elasticities of demand). Having obtained the Government's forecast of National Income over the next few years and made adjustments to this on the basis of other forecasting bodies' observations on the state of the U.K. economy, it excluded all those general categories which were unlikely to show a growth rate of real consumption of more than 7% per annum. These excluded categories of goods included, amongst others, foods of all kinds, most categories of industrial investment equipment and certain categories of consumer durable goods which were anticipated to have reached the approach to the saturation point (i.e. where the income consumption curve begins to grow at a falling rate). The categories of good which stood out as those where high rates of growth were anticipated included transport goods, some consumer electricals, packing industries, some distribution industries, some children's products and some products associated with housing, including do-it-yourself goods.

The team realised that in excluding markets which had a forecast growth rate of less than 7%, it would be excluding more narrowly defined product areas within these markets with higher growth rates than the minimum required, but it was considered that overall growth in the wider market category would provide some assurance.

This process of selection of general market areas was completed by the team's introducing an explicit constraint partly based on resources. This was that any product area chosen must be one which involved relatively small unit expenditure by the buyer (as it was held that the firm's management expertise, particularly on the distribution side, was more suited to this). This constraint the firm was prepared to drop if the appropriate opportunity came along. So in the areas of high growth, the firm selected for further investigation (to see if they were likely to satisfy the minimum requirements of the firm) the areas listed below together with the team's justification for the choice, any particular points of risk and assessment of difficulties in acquiring the required resources.

Car accessories : market growing in real terms at 11% per annum, distribution system for them already distributing some of the firm's products, some of the products using materials which were similar to those already used by the firm, relatively small items of expenditure, technology relatively simple, buyers relatively price inelastic in their demand, perhaps because of prestige associations. Disadvantages included the increasing amount of foreign competition, but the impact of this was thought to be limited because of the partially self-contained nature of the British market and the need for special fitting of some accessories to particular markets; the extent to which the car market was affected by government policy and sensitive to oil price rises. The resources that would need to be acquired if the firm were to enter this general market area would be greater technical ability in the case of some car parts, managerial familiarity with the motor industry and contacts with the appropriate distributors.

Consumer electricals : market growing in real terms at an estimated 10% per annum, again the distribution system already partially shared and again using many materials already used. Only the smaller items seemed to fit with the firm's constraint, and they particularly had the advantage of sharing distribution with kitchen utensils, although this might prove to be an insignificant advantage if the firm found itself squeezed out of the market by foreign competition, which was one of the major disadvantages of this market. In particular the smaller items were found to be heavily subject to foreign competition. A major disadvantage was the large effect of government action, particularly in the imposition of taxation. A further problem, which seemed to be peculiar to the U.K. market, was the quite substantial concentration of the distribution network, which meant that small firms could find themselves squeezed for lower prices. The resources that would have to be acquired included technical resources. Marketing resources presented less of a problem than with car accessories. Some possibility existed of co-operative agreements with other firms on the technical side, such that the more technical parts could be bought in.

Packing industries: market growing extremely fast, of the order of 16% a year, but with wild fluctuations in individual sectors according to the situation in the raw material markets because of the high proportion of the cost taken up by the raw material itself, together with the high flexibility of packers in adopting alternative methods as prices rise. The major disadvantage was that the firm had no major familiarity with the packaging industry, except as a customer. The disadvantages of the fluctuations might be overcome if the firm could avoid commitment to any one particular raw material, such as paper. Possibly a complete new management team would have to be acquired, as well as the required technical competence. The heavy capital investment required was also cited as a disadvantage.

Distribution industries: a more steady growth rate, of the order of 8%. The main reason for analysing this further was stability, since it was considered a possible low-risk complement to high-risk activities. The main problem here was the fact that, unless there was hope of acquiring a small chain, it would take a very long time to achieve the required expansion, because of the problems of site acquisition, etc. However, an advantage would be that if distribution outlets could be set up that carried some of the firm's existing products, then some costs might be saved. The resources that would need to be acquired were managerial expertise in distribution, the physical resources required to distribute, and the heavy initial capital required for stocking up.

Children's products: a very rapidly growing market in terms of value, since parents were buying more and more sophisticated toys for their children, while many other products were now no longer being made by the parents (e.g. clothes) but were being bought ready-made. The more durable products were seen as particularly suitable, because of the materials they used and because of some commonality of distribution characteristics. The main problem here was again the arrival of substantial foreign competition at low prices, but there was also the possibility of producing high-quality products which would have substantial market appeal. The good name of British products in this area was seen as a possible advantage as far as export potential was concerned. The main resource that would need to be acquired was familiarity with the marketing characteristics of these products.

Housing products : a market growing at a steady pace, with some sectors growing fast. The original fittings market was subject to severe economic fluctuations along with the housing market. Replacement fittings had a fairly steady market, in part of which the firm was already engaged. Further involvement here would mean broadening the firm's product range but also much deeper involvement with the original fitters. The major problem was the unstable state of the original equipment market. The main resource developments needed were managerial contacts with the construction industry and, if diversification into office fittings were considered, with office-fitting distributors and the fitting firms themselves.

Having selected these areas as those in which the possibilities *prima facie* seemed most promising, the next step was to investigate them in more detail. The activities of the team cannot be described in great detail here. But the most important point on which the team laid stress, before investigating the competitive situation, was the determination of the likely future rate of growth of demand in these areas, in particular whether there was any likelihood of saturation, which was seen as a major risk to a long-term product plan because of the possible slow rate of growth of the firm's own sales that would be associated with saturation.

Two areas were laid aside for the time being on the grounds of possible saturation. These were transport products and consumer electricals. It was recognised by the research team that this saturation might be delayed, but in the meantime the other areas were considered more likely to throw up profitable possibilities.

This left for consideration packing, distribution, children's products and housing products. The team considered this to be too wide an area to be investigated in detail, and therefore proceeded to an analysis of competitive advantage in the areas under consideration, with the qualification that any areas discarded at this stage would be continuously monitored. Any changes in the competitive position would be related to the firm's developing resource base and competitive position, and the decision reconsidered. The size of the firm's management team was not taken as a cast-iron constraint here, since if the team produced evidence that more areas were worth investigating than there were resources to investigate, serious consideration would be given to expanding the strength of the investigative team.

The analysis of competitive advantage produced the following result. Packing industries demanded a very high level of technical competence, working in extremely close contact with customers, a situation which could only be developed over several years. There were many firms already in the market, and there was strong import competition in the areas where packaging could itself be successfully packed for long-distance trading. Although there was considerable similarity in technology between some of the manufacturing machines and some of the machines used on the plastics side of the firm, there were also crucial areas of difference. The close levels of tolerance worked to in the industry due to the extensive automation of packing would ensure that the firm would be at a considerable disadvantage until the appropriate skills were acquired. The complete difference in customer base was also considered a serious disadvantage.

Given the very high investment that would have been necessary in order to sell at a competitive price (the economies of scale being high), the team decided that it was too risky to consider moving into this market. This left distribution, housing products and children's products.

The fragmented nature of competition in most distribution industries, dictated by the geographical dispersion of demand, meant that the idea of competitive advantage was difficult to use, even if the distribution industry were narrowly defined. In some sites, a given kind of shop would prosper, while in others it would not. The key competitive characteristics seemed to be size, which enabled many kinds of distributor to obtain substantial quantity discounts, and the management ability to locate suitable sites and plan appropriate sized outlets for them. It was considered that, with the acquisition of some management talent in this field, the firm could partly achieve its aims by expanding in this area. The firm's competitive advantage would be most in markets related to those of its current products, so the firm decided to investigate the possibilties of hardware distribution.

In housing products, the firm's advantage lay in products related to do-it-yourself products, i.e. fitments which could be fitted by the average householder. However, foreign competition looked like becoming too strong here, so some move away from the customer base was considered appropriate, into the area of direct supplying to construction companies, even if this involved associating the firm with construction cycles. Although the competition was quite strong here, no firm seemed to have attempted a concerted attack on a broad base. For the time being, this was out of the question as far as internal diversification was concerned, but considered feasible if suitable acquisitions were made. For the time being, the firm decided to concentrate on suiting some of its product range to the industry and on the possibility of introducing new ones.

The children's products market was highly competitive, but several companies had already obtained a very strong foothold by striking upon one product which was highly in demand and using that as a base for expansion. The firm was already used to doing this in its own industries, therefore this was considered to be a significant advantage, given the rapidly changing nature of demand in the market, which meant that new openings would be occurring all the time.

In considering the question of competitive advantage, the firm used the notions of resource, customer and product set in evaluating the likely freedom from competition by existing firms. In doing so it assumed, in an attempt to be realistic, that other firms' attitudes to moves away from their resource, product and customer bases would be less flexible than its own. It was therefore able to discount several major competitors in each case. The team found it difficult in some cases to set a limit to the number of possible competitive firms to be considered, so some more or less arbitrary decisions had to be taken here.

The next stage of analysis for the team was that of micro-demand estimation. Because of the descriptive detail necessary here, the analysis of only one of the product areas will be described from this point. The conclusions of the analysis for the other areas will be introduced towards the end of the analysis.

MICRO-DEMAND ESTIMATION FOR CHILDREN'S PRODUCTS

The first step here is to fix the characteristics of the new product or products. In order to do this, the team first of all defined the major categories of children's products as follows : clothing, toys, aids for mothers and non-durable products. On reconsideration of the firm's advantages relative to actual and possible competition, non-durable products and clothing were set aside as requiring technologies completely different from those already in use by the firm. These were to be reconsidered later as possible diversifications if the firm succeeded in the area.

The techniques described in Chapter 3 were then used to produce a mapping of requirements of consumers (in this case the mothers) and a ranking of the extent to which the known products already in this area satisfied these requirements. Since the team knew fairly well what sort of techniques could be employed here, they drew upon the expertise of consultants only for the calculations. This allowed the firm to identify gaps in the areas in question. Several gaps were identified, but as no measures were available to evaluate the depth of these gaps (in the sense of the intensity of need of consumers for the products), some simple pricing experiments were carried out on the basis of product descriptions in order to test this. The extent to which a given gap was worth considering was measured by a simple function of the number of people preferring a description to known products and the price premium which they indicated they would be prepared to pay. In the case where there was really no acceptable product, this premium was of course large.

Next, the team had to make some attempt to establish the stability of these parameters. This involved finding reasons for preferences (on which data had been collected in the descriptions preference test) and trying to predict the durability of these reasons. If the reason was simply that the products currently marketed were too highly priced, this was not estimated to be durable, since manufacturers of these products could simply change their pricing policy. But major deficiencies in design of existing products was considered to be a durable reason, since design changes cannot always be effected quickly, and the fact that a product has design deficiencies affects consumers' perceptions of it for some time in the future. Some attempt was also made to analyse the characteristics of preferrers. If they were found to be in low-income groups, the preference was considered unlikely to be durable on a national basis because of the steady growth of income, and the likely change in preferences of the current preferrers.

This analysis produced two major possibilities : a mother's aid, which we shall call product X, and an educational toy, which we shall call product Y. There were also several slightly less preferred specifications which the team put aside for consideration in case the costs of production of X and Y proved to be to high. The patterns of sales of similar products were examined (to the extent that any data were available) and it was noted that there was, if anything, a fairly long (10+ years) cycle attached to this kind of product, which would give the firm sufficient opportunity to use the product as a base for further launches.

The next step taken by the team was to invite the design staff to work on the product concepts. The problem here was that the design staff were so used to working in their accustomed areas that they had to bridge a considerable conceptual gap. First, they needed to familiarise themselves with the products currently on the market, both in the U.K. and overseas. Considerable surveying of the technical literature was also required, particularly on the safety side. A further problem was that many of the design staff had been used to sorting out problems presented to them by the marketing or production staff, and they found it difficult to fit this new assignment into their order of priorities without help from top management. This was the first positive response required from the firm other than those managers working on the team, so considerable stress was laid on being able to achieve a solution to the design problem without too much upheaval. Top management helped solve this problem by interceding with the production and marketing staff and asking for some holding back of less essential design work. At the same time, consideration was given to the expansion of the design staff that would inevitably have to occur if the products X and Y were actually considered produceable.

A simple design strategy was worked out. The designers were to attempt to produce three designs for both X and Y, a low-, a medium- and a high-cost design, the cost being roughly estimated on the basis of the materials used and the complexity of the item. Although the demand analysis had shown that there would be room for products of more than one quality level, the team did not consider it wise to examine the costs of producing combinations of product quality levels because this would be concentrating the risks of investment, which higher management was unlikely to accept until at least one new product in the area was shown to be successful.

On the basis of the preference testing, the firm then estimated the range within which unit sales would fall if prices were set at around the level for products of similar importance for the consumer (which was not easily measurable since the closeness of substitutes could not be determined). Within this range the firm then tried to estimate costs. Here there were two important problems, factory costs and promotional costs.

The actual manufacturing costs of the different varieties raised no problem when considered in isolation, because the technique to be used was fairly self-evident and did not show much in the way of changes of cost level within the range under consideration. The problem was where the new product would be produced if it were considered feasible. Both factories were running at or near to capacity on a shift-working basis. But the problems of expanding the London factory (which specialised in the plastics side) were considerable, and the designers had considered it infeasible to produce X and Y in anything but plastics. Although some spare capacity was likely to become available as the firm's market in kitchen utensils declined further, as was anticipated, this would be nothing like enough for the purposes of a major new product programme.

The Midland factory, on the other hand, was not so well suited to these products. Therefore consideration was given to the costs of staggering the introduction of the products until it was considered feasible (from the point of view of profitability) to open a green-field factory. This raised a difficult costing problem and also the question of product deletion to make space.

This problem caused the team to consider the need for a products deletion committee, but the major problem arose from the allocation of the costs of any rearrangement between existing products (some of which would benefit from the subsequent rearrangement) and the new products. Since it was very difficult to estimate the impact of any rearrangement on existing products, the firm decided to allocate the whole of the extra cost to any new products that might be decided upon, on the grounds that the extra costs would not have been incurred without them, with the reservation that the structure of costings would need to be reviewed after two years, when any new products would be in production in space taken over from old products, and after five years, when any new factory that might have proved necessary would have been built and in operation.

The costings of the different designs were therefore carried out on two assumptions, either with or without a new factory.

The promotional costs were very difficult to estimate. Since there were no published surveys of all promotional costs for the products in question, there was little way of estimating how sales might vary with promotional costs. The team therefore considered some of its own products which had a similar structure of distribution and estimated the kind of levels that would be required to get the products accepted into the outlets. But an arbitrary assumption had to be made, and a sensitivity analysis of the effect of this on total costs showed that as long as the estimate of the amount of promotional expenditure required to produce a given output was not out by more than 20%, the variation could safely be ignored.

The Finance Department had some problems in producing figures according to the specification required by the new products team, since the team wanted estimates of the true opportunity costs of each item of input rather than the appropriated or paid costs. This involved the Finance Department in some investigation of the origins and status of their figures and therefore caused some disruption of their normal procedures. But this was considered to be worth while because of the long-term benefits to the firm's product appraisal apparatus.

When the costs had been drawn up for each specification, price levels were hypothesised on the basis of the general demand analysis and the preference analysis, this time taking into account how low the price could go while still yielding the required rate of return on capital. In both cases, only the medium- and low-cost variants proved to be viable on this criterion, since the required margin over costs for the high-cost variants seemed likely to be realised only under the best of conditions. However, the high-cost variants were not put aside completely, but were simply deferred for consideration until more was known about the market through actually producing the products. In each case the firm chose the medium-cost variant, since this was considered more likely to be able to resist any low-price foreign competition and also to leave room for cost-cutting approximations to the low-cost model if the competitive situation should so require.

Having found that the medium-cost variants of both the mother's aid and the educational toy were worth producing, the firm then considered the risk aspects of producing both products at once. The team considered that, in order to spread risk, both products should not be produced at once. Rather, one should be held in reserve until the performance of the first had become clear. Since as far as the team was concerned there was nothing to choose between them, an arbitrary choice was made and the team decided to defer the mother's aid.

This analysis now had to be integrated with the results of the analysis of the other broad possibilities, housing products and distribution industries. In the housing products market, the team had shown that specialised light fittings would be an appropriate product area to enter, while in the distribution market, analysis had shown that the only possibility lay in taking over a small stores group which sold general merchandise. The latter was considered highly desirable by management, given the fairly good financial position of the firm and the fact that a particular group had already been located. Preliminary negotiations had suggested that a reasonable approach would be taken up. Such a diversification into distribution services would not raise the problem of factory space. This was however considered largely fortuitous.

The team now considered the problems of organising the two new product possibilities such that they became well integrated with the other activities of the firm. The product management structure in the Marketing Department seemed well suited to take the products, but initially at least the turnover might not be large enough to justify a full product team. Because of the special nature of the products, it was considered necessary to set up a new products department, with its own management structure, partly composed of managers transferred from elsewhere in the firm and partly of newly hired managers. It was considered essential to attach some designers specifically to this team because of the very different nature of the problems that they faced. It was considered that after a few years the department might be reabsorbed in the general management structure.

This left the question of the details of the marketing strategy to be decided. The principal problem for both the light fittings and the children's products was securing distribution. In the case of light fittings, the firm would have to make solid contacts with the trade, both constructors and sub-contractors, while for children's products, the main problem was to persuade distributors who were not already acquainted with the firm that the product was worth stocking. Since the firm did not have an established name in this area, this would mean extensive and expensive sales campaigns, combined with promotional discounts. But the firm was asked by the team to consider its whole distribution strategy very seriously in order to ascertain whether a more coherent approach over the whole product range, temporarily disjointed as it might seem, might be better than a piecemeal approach. This might involve attempting to persuade distributors who stocked none of the firm's products to try some of its products. In general, it was considered an appropriate time for re-evaluation in this area.

As already noted, the firm was not able to obtain much information on promotional expenditure for the children's products. It was considered necessary to rely on similiarities between its own products and the new products in order to estimate the required level of promotional expenditure, until the firm had more experience in this area.

The team stressed that its recommendations, which were carried out by the firm, should be kept constantly under review, that the consequences of the resource constraints in excluding certain possibilities should be registered and the appropriate decisions reassessed. When the final characteristics of the new products in production and sale were clear, the wisdom of the final choices would be more apparent, and the firm could then use information on discarded possibilities for the next stage of the new product plan. The constraints assumed should be listed together with the reasons for their adoption, and any change in the factors contributing to the rationale should be investigated.

POSTSCRIPT TO THE DECISIONS

The two products, the educational toy and the range of light fittings, were launched and the distribution group taken over within a three-year period. Because of the firm's strong connections with widely diversifying multiple and chain stores, making the initial contacts for the educational toy and persuading the distributors to experiment with stocking it did not present too much of a problem, given that the financial evaluation had shown that the firm was likely to be able to afford a reasonable level of publicity if the product were anything near as successful as the demand survey suggested it would be. Although the specialist dealers were all canvassed extensively, they were very apprehensive about taking a product of this kind from a producer with very little experience of the particular market in question. The firm considered that it would have to risk waiting until its position was established with the larger distributors. The highly seasonal nature of the trade made it likely that the firm could not be sure about this until at least a year and a half had elapsed from the launching date. Because during the first year after the launch sales did not seem to be going as well as had been forecast at the consumer level, given the strength of representation of the product in the distribution system, the firm considered ways of extending the appeal of the toy into an adult game, since the original research had shown that the principal buyers would be adults buying for children on special occasions. The toy was held to have substantial appeal as an adult game, and the design and promotion were altered accordingly, although the original version continued in production. This opened up the possibility of broadening the distribution network for the product into popular décor shops, in which the firm was already represented by some of its do-it-yourself products. This strategy proved to be successful, for the adult version of the game made substantial strides, and its success rubbed off onto the children's version, the educational value of which had become much clearer to would-be buyers among parents. At this final stage, the firm actively began to consider co-operation with other firms in this sector. Its lack of experience meant that much of its marketing effort was being carried out too expensively, but its familiarity with the materials needed and with some of the less usual methods of distribution were highly attractive to one or two smaller members of the educational supply and toy markets. The possibility of joint developments with firms of both kinds was being carefully looked into at the final stage of the investigation.

The light fitting presented much more substantial problems of long-term market development. Although some of the firm's products were at the time being sold through builders' merchants, more complete coverage of these outlets, together with obtaining some kind of franchise with firms responsible for installation, were major priorities. Considerable managerial effort was devoted to these ends. Substantial direct mailing of builders' merchants was undertaken, and the response here was strong enough for the firm to be able to decide to orientate its marketing campaign for the product more strongly towards the merchants, with less stress placed on the installers. The key problem, for both of these, was the demonstration of the ease of installation of the product. This had to be done through the standard exhibition circuit. Regional differences in installation practices, which still persisted to some extent, made the firm decide that a rolling launch might be suitable. This also fitted in with the strong initial demand on marketing resources that was being made by the children's product and the difficulty the firm was having in acquiring marketing staff of the required calibre and training them at the required speed. The firm therefore proceeded with the rolling launch. After a very long period during which it was not at all clear whether the launching of the product was justified, the profits derived from it reached an acceptable level. This was partly because the construction of new buildings suddenly turned downwards. However, apart from this, it became clear to the firm that the line could not be justified by itself, so that unless further products in the immediate market area could be developed, thus enabling the firm to spread the heavy marketing costs, the product would have to be withdrawn in the long run or sold to a firm with stronger representation in the area. The firm, given its need to expand, therefore embarked on a substantial research programme to see what other product possibilities might be acceptable in the market area.

The general merchandise stores group with which the firm had already had discussions showed itself willing to accept a part cash/part share-exchange offer. Although this meant a temporary reduction in Integrated Products' earnings on capital, this was not considered to be a serious handicap because evaluation of the group's prospects had been favourable. The conclusion concerning the worthwhileness of the investment depended to some extent, however, on some reorganisation within the group. This was for two reasons. The group had attained its present expansion through rather haphazard acquisition of sites. Some kind of rationalisation was necessary in order for the group to realise its full potential. The management structure of the group itself needed some changing in order for it to be able to carry out this task. Secondly, the number of products stocked by shops in the group was over the economical number, so some attention needed to be given to the rationalisation of lines. Because Integrated Products itself did not have all the necessary experience to achieve this, a comprehensive programme of management development was initiated. It was considered essential that this be done by internal management development rather than by hiring, since this would best ensure the long-term future of the management team.

By year +5, Integrated Products had achieved the launch of the two major product changes and had acquired the stores group. The financial figures for the firm were then as follows (figures in £000's) :

Sales	65,000
Capital employed	40,000
Gross profit	6,000
Depreciation	1,000
Taxation	1,900
Net profit	3,100
Rate of return on capital, net	7·8%
Employment (000's)	6·0

The fall in the net rate of return on capital had been anticipated as a consequence of heavy initial investment and of the acquisition of the

stores group, whose rate of return had been running at about 8%
before its acquisition. The next five years were to see the firm con-
solidate its position and achieve the ten-year sales and profit targets.

CONCLUSIONS

In this brief summary of the integrated approach to product planning
as applied in practice, we have tried to show in more down-to-earth
terms what it looks like when a firm proceeds with its product policy
according to the recommendations contained in this book. The limitations of the method are clear. There are several stages in the model
where fairly arbitrary limitations have to be introduced, although they
would not appear to be so arbitrary to the practising manager. The
stagewise approach which is dictated by the limited search and information-gathering resources of the firm means the possible exclusion of
new product projects which might prove to be highly beneficial to the
firm. But the crucial point, which is stressed throughout this book, is
that as long as the process of product planning is regarded as an integrated whole and carried out according to a clearly conceived set of
aims, it becomes much easier to trace the consequences of assumptions
which may turn out to be unjustified, the origins of problems in the
system, and so on. It also makes it far easier for the firm to integrate
its overall corporate strategy with product planning. Corporate strategy
itself should start with precisely the same kind of search procedure that
initiates the product-planning process.

If a firm does not yet consider its product planning in terms as 'pre-
meditated' as those which define the discussion in this book, its managers should be able to get at least some idea of the implications of product policy for the rest of its activities, both in the short and long term.
Many firms will be unable to use some of the techniques mentioned in
this book, but it is hoped that they may at least derive some ideas about
how to arrange their product policy other than by starting with an
inventory of the firm's resources. Students of management should
actively consider what other forecasting and costing procedures might
usefully be adapted for product planning under the model discussed
in this book. If the book provokes some non-routine thought on the
matter, even if this results in a rejection of its conclusions, then it will
have succeeded in its purpose.

Notes

Chapter 1

1 Throughout this book, the term 'product' is taken to include service products.
2 If the annual capital input (however calculated) into a product is defined as k and actual annual sales are s, then the rate of return on capital r is equal to sy/k, where y is the profit margin on sales. If s/k is constant, then r is constant if y is constant.
3 For such an approach see E. A. Pessemier, *New Product Decisions: an analytical approach* (New York, 1966).

Chapter 2

1 See, for example, W. J. Baumol, *Economic Theory and Operations Analysis*, 2nd ed. (Englewood Cliffs, N. J., 1965) pp. 295ff.
2 Technically, this situation is referred to as an *uncertain* situation, which is defined as one in which it is not possible to calculate objective probabilities. Since in the area of product planning this is nearly always the case, the terms 'risk' and 'uncertainty' are used interchangeably in this book.
3 'The financing of corporations', in E. S. Mason (ed.), *The Corporation in Modern Society* (Harvard, 1959) p. 170.
4 The term 'satisficing' was used to best effect in R. M. Cyert and J. G. March, *A Behavioural Theory of the Firm* (Englewood Cliffs, N. J., 1963).
5 Note that without a clear definition of what is meant by short run and long run, this statement can be vacuous.
6 A paper by Stephen King, published in *Creating and Marketing New Products*, edited by G. Wills *et al.*, (London, 1973) pp. 65–96, discusses the question of diverse company objectives and the problem that they pose for the consultant. King points out that one of the most common objectives passed down the line is a purely financial one, but that this is very little help to the development personnel. In fact, he says, from middle management downwards, employees do not act as if the sole purpose of the company is to make profits. Instead, they act as if corporate objectives are to strengthen and preserve the continuity of the company, as well as the continuity of its products. This being so, it does not make too much sense to set objectives for development in purely economic terms. The objectives, he says, must be set in terms of the sort of business the company should go into in order to strengthen the personality or nature of the company and to tie in with the motives of the people working in it. Profit objectives fall naturally into place as criteria of the success of development. If firms did this, the consultants' job of course would be that much easier. But the really crucial question of what sorts of business the firm wants to go into or remain

in still needs to be discussed. Managers' commitments can in practice be changed to encompass different product areas, so they cannot be taken to be the defining rule for product planning.

7   See for example H. I. Ansoff, *Corporate Strategy*, (Penguin, 1968) Ch. 5.

8   This assumption is built into the theoretical basis of linear programming.

Chapter 3

1   The term 'demand area' is used here rather than 'market' because the latter term often implies that a fairly well-established demand already exists and is at least partly catered for. In other words, a market is defined by both supply and demand characteristics. The term 'demand area' is chosen to indicate that our concern here is entirely with consumer preferences.

2   In the research for this book, frequent examples were found of firms entering new markets by arranging for other firms to supply the new product or parts of it, either initially or permanently. Often there will be *some* ground which is common between the firm's existing products and a product launched in this way, but this may sometimes be lost as the firm finds other ways of organising itself to handle the new product. For example, the product might initially be introduced with the help of the other firm because of shared distributional characteristics, but the firm may later find better ways of distributing the product which differ from those used by its existing products.

3   Note that there is no assumption that the criteria adopted in each time period will necessarily be the same. It is of the essence of the satisficing process that the criteria used in screening possibilities are related to the aspirations of managers, which will change according to the state of the economy, the performance of the firm's products, etc.

4   The notion of 'survival' is a slightly problematic one, since in cases where the firm is taken over it normally still survives in the sense that most of its products continue to be sold and most of the managers and workers remain in their positions. Here we define survival as meaning the continuity of the product line of the firm and the success of any products that might be marketed by existing management.

5   For an approach which supports the claim that far more information gathering is necessary, see W. R. King and D. I. Cleland, 'Environmental Systems for Strategic Marketing Planning', *Journal of Marketing*, 38 (Oct 1974) 35–40. This paper describes an information system for providing externally generated data to support strategic marketing planning. The basic idea is that it is worth while developing information systems which support strategic planning, however difficult this may be.

6   This equating of consumption demand with the interest of consumer goods producers and of investment demand with the interest of industrial goods consumers is a convenient simplification. Of course, stocks of consumer goods and semi-finished goods are also effectively investments.

7   A guide to standard regression techniques can be found in any good statistics text. See, for example, F. E. Croxton *et al.*, *Applied General Statistics*, 3rd ed. (London, 1968), Chs. 19ff. This text also gives a useful introduction to time series analysis (Chs. 11ff).

8   For a description of this work and its relation to demand for transport, see R. Quandt, *The Demand for Travel, Theory and Measurement* (London, 1971).

9 For a good summary of the work in this area, see A. D. Shocker *et al.*, 'Towards the improvement of product search and screening', in *Marketing Involvement in Society and Economy*, ed. P. R. McDonald (American Marketing Association, 1969) pp. 168–175.

10 V. Stefflre, 'Market Structure Studies: New products for old markets and new markets for old products', in F. Bass *et al.*, *Application of the Sciences in Marketing* (New York, 1968) pp. 251–268.

Chapter 4

1 Booz, Allen and Hamilton, Inc., *The Management of New Products* (New York, 1960) pp. 5–6.

2 See, for example, A. Wilson, *The Assessment of Industrial Markets* (London, 1968), p. 21, R. N. White, 'How to use the "product life cycle" in marketing decisions', *Business Management* (Feb 1962) 74 and C. W. Randle, 'Selecting the research programme', *California Management Review*, II, 2 (1960) 10.

3 A. Patton, 'Top management's stake in a product's life cycle', *The Management Review* (Jun 1969) 4.

4 L. Fisher, *Industrial Marketing* (London, 1969) p. 92.

5 T. Levitt, 'Exploit the product life cycle', *Harvard Business Review* (Nov–Dec 1965) 88.

6 R. Polli, *A Test of the Classical Product Life Cycle by Means of Actual Sales Histories* (Ann Arbor, Michigan : University Microfilms, 1968), pp 4–12 (abbreviated here as *A Test*). The results of some of his research into non-durable products is summarised in R. Polli and V. Cook, 'Validity of the product life cycle', *Journal of Business*, 42, 4 (Oct 1969) 385–400 (abbreviated here as *Validity*).

7 Fisher, *Industrial Marketing*, p. 103.

8 Fisher, *Industrial Marketing*, p. 90.

9 Polli's work is the most comprehensive study of the empirical status of the product cycle, though the empirical testing is confined to the sales aspect and does not cover the trend in profit margins. As we note in the text, the breadth of his study necessitates the adoption of definitions of the cycle and of classes of product which are generally applicable. For an interesting example of how definitions may differ for specific applications, see W. E. Cox, Jr., 'Product life cycles as marketing models', *Journal of Business*, 40, 4 (Oct 1967) 375–384. In this article, the stages of the life cycle of ethical drugs are defined partly in relation to the length of time for which the drug appears in the catalogue of the firm or in the *Drug Topics Red Book*. Thus the introduction phase is defined as that between the catalogue birth of a product and its commercial birth (defined as when it reaches a national sales volume of 5000 new prescriptions a month).

10 Polli, *A Test*, pp. 70–72.

11 For details of the procedure, see Polli, *Validity*, pp. 393–394.

12 Polli, *A Test*, p. 224.

13 Even a relatively straightforward econometric approach can yield useful results. For example, K. Brockhoff, in 'A test for the product life cycle', *Econometrica*, 35, 3–4 (Jul–Oct 1967) 472–484, sets up an equation to explain the time distribution of sales of a German car company. Excluding cases in which capacity limitations had produced basically rectangular sales curves (and this brings out an important point about the extent to which

sales curves are determined by supply considerations), Brockhoff found a good fit for the equation

$$S_t = at^b e^{-ct} + dR_t$$

where S_t = sales in time period t,

R_t = sum of sales of related products sold by the same company (thus allowing for substitution between the products of the company),

t = time and a, b, c and d are parameters to be estimated. The fact that the equation gave a reasonable fit does not indicate a definite interpretation by itself, but the relative simplicity of the fitted function is encouraging. However, if the form of the equation is to be considered useful, it needs to be tested more extensively in other product areas.

Chapter 5

1   For a more comprehensive discussion of design and development problems, see for example C. Hearn Buck, *Problems of Product Design and Development* (London, 1963).

2   For a good summary of the role of creativity in innovation, see W. H. Reynolds, *Products and Markets* (New York, 1969), Ch. 3. One method of product design which tries to make the role of creativity more certain is suggested by E. M. Tauber, in 'Discovering new product opportunities with problem inventory analysis', *Journal of Marketing*, 39, 1 (Jan 1975) 67–70. This approach tries to make the relation between demand characteristics and design more certain.

3   See, for example, J. Jewkes *et al.*, *The Sources of Invention* (London, 1958) and J. Langrish *et al.*, *Wealth through Knowledge*, (London, 1972).

4   For a description of the role of calculus in any maximising decision, see any micro-economics text-book, for example, W. J. Baumol, *Economic Theory and Operations Analysis*, (Englewood Cliffs, N. J., 1965), 2nd ed, Ch. 4.

5   The term 'market imperfection' in economics is used to describe a situation in which any one agent (be it buyer, seller, distributor or government) significantly influences the amount of a commodity sold or bought or the price at which transactions take place. This, of course, applies to most situations.

6   Group technology is the production of goods by workers working in small groups, each worker doing several jobs, as opposed to mass production, where workers repeat the same action and are not responsible for the outcome in any significant sense.

Chapter 6

1   Mathematical programming is a general term designed to cover calculations which require several steps. In economics and marketing the techniques of mathematical programming are particularly useful in selecting one or a few possibilities out of many, according to certain criteria. The basis of the techniques is that they provide rules for deleting and including possibilities from the set under consideration.

2   The internal rate of return of a project is defined as that rate of interest which will reduce the net present value of the project to zero. In principle, for a capital investment project, if the internal rate of return is greater than

the cost of borrowed funds, the project is worth undertaking for a firm that
aims to maximise profits.
3 See, for example, B. M. Richman, 'A rating scale for product innovation',
   Business Horizons (Summer 1962) 37–44.

Chapter 7

1 By 'true test marketing' is meant the actual launch of the product on to a
   restricted section of the market, as opposed to concept testing or prototype
   placement, etc.
2 A useful summary of the evolution of distribution system characteristics is
   given in N. Kaldor, 'The economic aspects of advertising', *Review of Economic Studies* (1950–51), XVIII, 1–27.
3 'Market segmentation' is a method of marketing analysis which divides up
   the market into different 'segments' according to certain important characteristics (such as income, age, etc.) on the hypothesis that these characteristics are important determinants of market behaviour.
4 See, for example, A. Wilson, *The Assessment of Industrial Markets* (London, 1968).
5 See Science Policy Research Unit, University of Sussex, *Success and Failure in Industrial Innovation* (Centre for the Study of Industrial Innovation, 1972).
6 See R. H. Offord, *Product Management in Action* (London, 1967).
7 See J. Woodward, *Industrial Organisation* (London, 1965).

Bibliography

L. Abbott, *Quality and Competition* (New York, 1955).

H. I. Ansoff, *Corporate Strategy* (New York, 1965).

J. S. Bain, *Barriers to New Competition* (Harvard, 1956).

W. J. Baumol, *Economic Theory and Operations Analysis*, 2nd ed. (Englewood Cliffs, N.J., 1965).

T. L. Berg and A. Schuchman (eds.), *Product Strategy and Management* (New York, 1963).

A. Bevan, 'The U.K. potato crisp industry 1960–72: a study in new entry competition', *Journal of Industrial Economics* (Jun 1974).

Booz, Allen and Hamilton, Inc., *The Management of New Products* (New York, 1960).

Brand, Gruber and Co. (eds.), *The Professionals Look at New Products* (Michigan, 1969).

K. Brockhoff, 'A test for the product life cycle', *Econometrica*, 35, 3–4 (Jul–Oct 1967) 375–384.

E. Brunner, 'A note on potential competition', *Journal of Industrial Economics* (Jul 1961) 248–251.

C. H. Buck, *Problems of Product Design and Development* (London, 1963).

T. M. Burns and G. M. Stalker, *The Management of Innovation* (London, 1961).

W. F. Butler and R. A. Kavesh (eds.), *How Business Economists Forecast* (Englewood Cliffs, N.J., 1966).

R. D. Buzzell and R. E. M. Nourse, *Product Innovation in Food Processing 1954–64* (Harvard, 1967).

W. E. Cox, Jr., 'Product life cycles as marketing models', *Journal of Business*, 40, 4 (Oct 1967) 375–384.

F. E. Croxton *et al.*, *Applied General Statistics*, 3rd ed. (London, 1968).

M. T. Cunningham and M. A. A. Mammouda, 'Product strategy for industrial goods', *Journal of Management Studies*, 6, 2 (May 1969) 223–242.

R. M. Cyert and J. G. March, *A Behavioural Theory of the Firm* (Englewood Cliffs, N.J., 1963).

L. Fisher, *Industrial Marketing* (London, 1969).

L. N. Goslin, *The Product Planning System* (Homewood, Illinois, 1967).

D. C. Hague, *Pricing in Business* (London, 1971).

J. Jewkes *et al.*, *The Sources of Invention* (London, 1958).

S. C. Johnson and C. Jones, 'How to organise for new products', *Harvard Business Review* (May–Jun 1957) 49–62.

N. Kaldor, 'The economic aspects of advertising', *Review of Economic Studies*, XVIII (1950–51) 1–27.

A. D. H. Kaplan *et al.*, *Pricing in Big Business* (Washington, D.C., The Brookings Institution, 1958).

S. R. King, *Developing New Brands* (London, 1973).

W. R. King and D. I. Cleland, 'Environmental systems for strategic marketing planning', *Journal of Marketing*, 38 (Oct 1974) 35–40.

P. Kotler, 'Phasing out weak products', *Harvard Business Review* (Mar–Apr 1965) 69–80.

J. Langrish *et al.*, *Wealth from Knowledge* (London, 1972).

R. Leduc, *How to Launch a New Product* (London, 1966).

T. Levitt, 'Exploit the product life cycle', *Harvard Business Review*, 43 (Nov–Dec 1965).

J. W. Lorsch, *Product Innovation and Organisation* (New York, 1965).

D. J. Luck, *Product Policy and Strategy* (Englewood Cliffs, N.J., 1972).

P. R. McDonald (ed.), *Marketing Involvement in Society and Economy* (American Marketing Association, 1969).

R. Marris, *The Economic Theory of Managerial Capitalism* (London, 1964).

P. Marvin, *Product Planning Simplified* (American Marketing Association, 1970).

E. S. Mason (ed.), *The Corporation in Modern Society* (Harvard, 1959).

R. S. Mason, 'Price and product quality assessment', *European Journal of Marketing* (Spring 1974) 29–41.

D. Maynard Phelps (ed.), *Product Management: Selected Readings 1960–69* (American Marketing Association, 1970).

J. E. Meade, 'The optimal balance between economies of scale and variety of products: an illustrative model', *Economica*, 41, 164 (Nov 1974) 359–367.

J. Morley (ed.), *Launching a New Product* (London, 1968).

L. Nabseth and G. F. Ray, *The Diffusion of New Industrial Processes: an International Study* (Cambridge, 1974).

R. H. Offord, *Product Management in Action* (London, 1967).

J. H. Parfitt and B. J. K. Collins, 'Use of consumer panels for brand share prediction', *Journal of Marketing Research* (May 1968) 131–146.

A. Patton, 'Top management's stake in a product's life cycle', *The Management Review* (Jun 1959).

E. Penrose, *The Theory of the Growth of the Firm* (Oxford, 1963).

E. A. Pessemier, *New Product Decisions: An Analytical Approach* (New York, 1966).

J. Pilditch *et al.*, *The Business of Product Design* (London, 1965).

R. Polli, *A Test of the Classical Product Life Cycle by Means of Actual Sales Histories* (Ann Arbor, Michigan, University Microfilms, 1968).

R. Polli and V. Cook, 'Validity of the product life cycle', *Journal of Business*, 42, 4 (Oct 1969) 385–400.

R. Quandt, *The Demand for Travel: Theory and Measurement* (London, 1971).

C. W. Randle, 'Selecting the research programme', *California Management Review*, II, 2 (1960).

W. H. Reynolds, *Products and Markets* (New York, 1969).

B. M. Richman, 'A rating scale for product innovation', *Business Horizons* (Summer 1962) 37–44.

E. M. Rogers, *The Diffusion of Innovation*, 2nd ed. (New York, 1971).

B. Sandkull, *On Product Changes and Product Planning* (Swedish Institute of Administrative Research, 1968).

Science Policy Research Unit (University of Sussex), *Success and Failure in Industrial Innovation* (Centre for the Study of Industrial Innovation, 1972).

A. D. Shocker *et al.*, 'Towards the improvement of product search and screening', in P. R. McDonald, *Marketing Involvement*, pp. 168–175.

V. Stefflre 'Market structure studies: New products for old markets and new markets for old products', in F. Bass *et al.*, *Application of the Sciences in Marketing* (New York, 1968), pp. 251–268.

E. M. Tauber, 'Discovering new product opportunities with problem inventory analysis', *Journal of Marketing*, 39, 1 (Jan 1975) 67–70.

C. A. Wainwright and J. T. Gerlach, *Successful Management of New Products* (New York, 1968).

R. N. White, 'How to use the "product life cycle" in marketing decisions', *Business Management* (Feb 1962).

G. Wills, *Technological Forecasting* (London, 1972).

G. Wills *et al.* (eds.), *Creating and Marketing New Products* (London, 1973).

A. Wilson, *The Assessment of Industrial Markets* (London, 1968).

W. Woods, 'The development and measurement of new product concepts, in Brand, Gruber and Co., *Professionals Look at New Products*.

J. Woodward, *Industrial Organisation, Theory and Practice* (London, 1965).

Index